HEINEMANN
NEW WINDMILLS

BUDDY'S SONG

Buddy is depressed. His dad is in prison and Buddy feels it's his fault, and his mum is busy with her new job. Then Buddy picks up a guitar, begins to sing, and by the time his dad comes home he's ready to perform! His dad, the fun-loving Buddy Holly fan who is more of an adolescent than his own son, has great plans for Buddy. But Buddy has to think about what he really wants.

ABOUT THE AUTHOR

Nigel Hinton was born and brought up in London. He worked in advertising before becoming a teacher and an actor. He has written three books for young children, four for teenagers and one for adults. His books have been translated into many languages. He has also written for TV, including the highly successful 5-part serial of *Buddy*.

He is married, and lives in Kent. His main interests are rock music, especially the work of Bob Dylan, swimming and films.

Buddy's Song

Nigel Hinton

HEINEMANN
NEW WINDMILLS

Heinemann Educational Publishers
Halley Court, Jordan Hill, Oxford OX2 8EJ
Part of Harcourt Education

Heinemann is the registered trademark of Harcourt Educational Limited

ISBN 0 435 12338 6

First published in 1987 by J. M. Dent & Sons Ltd

First published in the New Windmill Series 1989

04 05 06 07 08 09 19 18 17 16 15 14

Cover illustration by Beverly Levy

Printed in the UK by Clays Ltd, St Ives plc

1

The first time Buddy visited his dad in prison was a disaster. His mum had already been a couple of times on her own because she said it would be best if he didn't go until his dad got used to being there. Buddy had agreed – partly because he thought his mum and dad ought to have time to talk things over on their own, and partly because he was scared. He missed his dad like mad, but what would it be like to see him locked up and dressed in prison clothes?

His mum had cried after the first visit and said that his dad was really low and miserable, but after the second visit she said that he'd cheered up a lot and that he wanted to see Buddy. A week later, the visiting order came. It was made out to Carol Clark and Buddy Clark and it said that the visit was for two o'clock the following Saturday.

Buddy found it hard to get to sleep on Friday night. He lay in bed trying to imagine what it would be like. What would they talk about? Should he say he was sorry, or would it be best not to mention things like that and just try to make his dad happy by telling him that he was working hard at school and that he was doing well? He wouldn't tell him about the horrible things some of the other kids had said when they'd read the report in the local paper. One of the boys in his class had cut out the headline 'Teddy Boy Thief Gets Eighteen Months' and pinned it on the noticeboard in his classroom. Buddy had found out that it was Clive Tiernon and they'd had a fight in the corridor and Mr. Normington had caught them and stopped them – but not before Buddy had landed a good punch on Tiernon's nose and made it bleed. No, he mustn't mention any of that.

He would just talk about good things like how he was looking after his dad's Harley-Davidson, taking it out of the shed and oiling and polishing it and making sure it would be ready for him when he came out of prison. And about how he was helping his mum with her Business exams, and how he was helping her decorate the house and make it look nice.

Those things would be easy to talk about, but one question kept him turning restlessly in bed, unable to fall asleep. Did his dad blame him for everything? Before he'd gone to prison he'd told Buddy that it was his own fault that he'd got into trouble and that Buddy had only been trying to help, but perhaps he'd changed his mind now that he was actually locked up in a cell. There was an old Elvis Presley song that his dad used to listen to and that Buddy had kept playing recently. It was called 'I Want to Be Free' and it was about a man in prison looking out of a window and wishing he could be free like a bird in a tree. Perhaps that's how his dad felt, and perhaps he hated him because he was the one who had caused him to be caught.

The night passed terribly slowly. His heart fluttered and lurched, sending waves of heat to his face whenever he thought about it. And the more he tried not to think about it, the more it came back. He was like a fish on a hook, continually being pulled back no matter how hard he tried to swim away. And the mad thing was that part of him was the fish and part of him was the fisherman. Why was he always being torn in half like that? Sometimes it seemed to him he wasn't just one person but as though there were hundreds of different people locked up inside his head. Locked up – just like his dad in prison.

He saw the sky begin to grow light and then he must have fallen asleep because the next thing he knew it was day and his mum was calling up to him saying that it was late and that they had to go. All he wanted to do was sink back into sleep and forget everything, but he dragged himself out of bed and started to dress.

The prison was forty-five miles away. They had to catch a coach to Etchford and then a train to Atterbury. There were huge road-works just outside Etchford and the coach was held up for a quarter of an hour in the long tail-back of traffic so they had to run down the hill from the coach station and only just managed to catch the train. His mum's make-up was all messed up and she sat on the jolting train holding a small mirror, trying to do the mascara on her eyelashes. The brush slipped a couple of times and made smudges on her eyelids.

"Damn! I'll look a right mess for him," she said as she tried to wipe away the smears with a paper hankie.

Suddenly, Buddy's eyes watered at the thought of his mum trying to make herself look nice for his dad, and he turned away and looked out of the window. The train was rolling through hilly countryside and every so often they passed isolated houses. The sun was shining and people were out doing ordinary Saturday things – washing cars, digging the garden, painting their houses or just standing around talking. In one garden they roared past he saw a young boy kicking a ball to his dad, just like Buddy and his dad used to do. If only they could do it now. If only. That was a game he played all the time.

If only he hadn't found out that his dad was stealing. If only he hadn't told the police about 56 Croxley Street where the stolen goods were kept. If only his dad had stayed at home as he was supposed to, instead of turning up at 56 just when the police arrived. If only. It could go on for ever. If only he had never been born. If only the world had never started. But that game never got you anywhere, never changed a thing. He had been born. He had tried to help his dad. And it had all gone wrong and his dad had been caught. A[illegible] wasn't playing football with his dad. He was on a tra[illegible]ng to visit him in prison.

They got to Atterbury at twenty to one and went to a café. Buddy had a glass of orange juice but he couldn't eat a thing. He even felt sick watching his mum trying to eat a pizza. She cut it into small pieces then began pushing the bits round the plate with her fork. She ate two pieces, then put the fork down.

"I'm not hungry either," she said, pushing the plate away. "Come on, let's go."

They walked slowly up the hill and a shadow came racing towards them as a cloud covered the sun. They turned a corner and there, ahead of them, was the high grey wall of the prison. Behind the wall stood dark buildings with rows and rows of barred windows. Black smoke was pouring out of a tall chimney stack. It was as grim and terrible as Buddy had ever imagined – and that was where his dad was spending eighteen months.

His whole chest shook with the throbbing of his heart as they stood in front of the big wooden gates and his mum reached out and rang the bell. All he wanted to do was turn and run, run far away and not have to go through with it. In a daze, he saw the small door open in the large gates. He saw his mum step through and he followed. The door slammed behind them and there was a jingling of keys and the clang of a lock being turned.

He stared at the back of his mum's coat as they walked up the three steps to the reception. He watched as the man behind the counter slid open the glass and took the visiting order. He saw the man stamp the paper and hand it back to his mum. Then he followed her as she turned and went down the steps into the corridor again.

Buddy's heart was pounding, and when they stopped in front of the iron-barred gate that led into the main courtyard his knees began to tremble. There was more jingling of keys and another clunk of a lock, then the doors swung open and his mum stepped through into the main courtyard. He noticed how bright and lively her reddish hair looked against the dark, dingy building in front of them. He hadn't moved. His knees were shaking and his feet were too heavy to lift. He saw his mum turn and look at him. She lifted her hand slightly. He shook his head and his breath shuddered inside his lungs.

"Come on, Buddy," she said, taking a step back towards him.

"No." It was the one word he could think of.

She looked away in the direction of the dark building, then looked back. "What'll he think?"

Buddy shook his head and looked down. He heard his mum saying something quietly to the man at the gate then he heard her footsteps go away. The gate clanged shut and the keys jingled and a lock closed, then the man put his arm round his shoulder and led him back down the corridor. They turned left into a room and the man sat him down on a chair.

"You can wait here," he said. "Don't worry – lots of people find it hard. You'll be all right."

The man went away and Buddy stared down at the orangey-red plastic of the seat between his legs. He saw the tiny bobbles of the plastic and the little ridged scar left by a cigarette burn. His head was pounding and shivers kept running up and down his back.

People came into the room and talked and waited, then went away when someone called their names. There was a sickly smell of cigarette smoke and the floor at his feet was covered with ash and stubs. Then he saw a tear splash on his shoe. More people came in and sat opposite him. A little girl whispered, "That boy's crying," and there was a "shush" sound from her parents.

He didn't care. He stared at the floor and saw the tears fall and all he could think of was his dad.

A long time later there was a shuffling next to him and his mum's voice said, "Buddy, it's me. Come on, we're going home." He felt her pull his elbow to make him stand up but he shook her hand away, brushed his face with his sleeve, and stood up on his own. He followed her out of the room and along the corridor. The wooden door was opened and he stepped outside.

The sky was overcast and the streets were wet with rain. They walked fast to the station but found that they had just missed their train and had to wait for forty minutes for the next one.

"Was he angry?" Buddy finally managed to say as they sat on the bench and looked at the rain falling on the glistening rails.

"No," his mum said.

"What did he say?"

"He was disappointed, that's all."

They didn't say anything else all the way home.

Four days later Buddy got home from school and found a letter lying on the mat. It was addressed to him. It was from his dad. He went upstairs to his bedroom and sat down on the bed before he opened it. There was the name of the prison printed at the top of the sheet and, below, his dad's scrawly writing.

Dear Buddy,
Please come and see me. Don't be ashamed of me.
Love, Dad.

He didn't cry. He wouldn't let himself cry. He picked up the photo of his dad from the top of his chest of drawers. Then he got down on his knees. He always felt awkward about prayers and things like that but he knew he needed to do something special. He held the photo out in front of him and looked at his dad's face. Never, ever again would he let his dad think he was ashamed of him. Never. He would do anything his dad wanted. He could never make things up to him but from now on he would do everything he could to make him happy.

He closed his eyes and said out loud, "I swear to God."

He opened his eyes and he knew that he had done something he could never go back on. He had made a vow.

2

The following weekend Buddy decided to paint the front door. His mum had been asking him to do it for nearly a month but he hadn't wanted to because it would mean covering the fingermarks near the lock. His dad had made them one day when his hands had been oily from the Harley-Davidson, and every time Buddy got back from school and slipped the key into the lock it reminded him of his dad and made him feel happier.

It was strange how little things like that had become important. He had even taken one of his dad's T-shirts out of the laundry basket the day after the trial. It was creased and a bit grimy but he had hidden it away in his cupboard behind all his old toys and games on the bottom shelf. Every so often he took it out and held it and looked at the words printed on it – 'Buddy Holly Lives' – and it was as though he was near his dad. It was crazy, but he didn't care. He liked to have it in his room and he didn't want it washed.

He couldn't make sense of these kinds of feelings. Was he the only one in the world with ideas like this in his head or did everyone else – all those people out there who looked so normal – did they all have the same sort of strange, secret thoughts? His mum certainly didn't seem to care the same way as he did about the things in the house. She had even suggested taking down the photos and posters of Buddy Holly that his dad had pinned on the wall above the record player. But he had got really upset and said that it was his dad's special corner, so she had agreed to leave them there.

The door was not as important as the photos, though, and he knew it would please his mum, so on the Saturday morning he washed all the greasemarks off and sand-papered the chipped paint until it was smooth. Then they went to the shop together and chose a dark green paint and bought a big paintbrush. After lunch Buddy started the first coat. He had nearly finished when he heard a footstep behind him. Turning, he saw Des King coming up the path. It was such a shock that Buddy stood up fast and almost knocked the paint over. Des King stopped and, for a moment, they looked at each other and Buddy felt a blush creep up his throat to his cheeks.

"Well," King said, taking off his glasses and breaking into a smile, "it's Buddy. The man of the house, now, are you? That's what I like to see. Is your mum in?"

Buddy bent down and laid the paintbrush across the top of the can to give himself a moment to think. What did King want? He was all smiles and his voice sounded friendly but you could never tell with him. The smile could freeze suddenly and that voice could turn angry without warning – Buddy still remembered how it had sounded when his dad had told King that he wanted to stop stealing. King had shouted and threatened him. That had been the day when Buddy had first thought of the plan to phone the police and tip them off about the stolen goods in 56 Croxley Street. Did he know that the plan had been meant to trap him?

"Well, is she?" King asked, and Buddy stood up and nodded. "Good, I'd like to see her."

The smile was still there and the voice was still friendly, but it was an order. Buddy turned and pushed the door.

"Mind your paint," King called, and then laughed as Buddy pulled his fingertips away and looked at the green paint all over them.

"Mum?" he shouted quickly, to cover his embarrassment.

His mum was at the sink doing some washing. She glanced over her shoulder, saw Des King, and pushed down heavily on the jeans she was washing. She kept her hands there, plunged deep into the suds as if she were leaning on them for support. Then, slowly, she pulled them out, rinsed them under the tap, and picked up a towel from the draining-board. Buddy noticed how red her hands were and how a thread from the towel snagged on her wedding ring and stuck there.

King raised his hand and smiled but his smile was less cocky and sarcastic than it had been outside. He twirled his glasses in the other hand and then put them on and folded his arms. He actually looked nervous, and when Buddy sneaked a glance at his mum he could see why – her face was set hard and there was nothing welcoming or frightened about it.

"Hello, Carol," King said. "The place looks nice. See your boy's helping you."

"What do you want, Des?" Her voice sounded as if she were bored and slightly irritated by the interruption.

"Just a little chat." King tried another smile.

"What have you got to say?"

King nodded towards Buddy. "Not in front of the boy."

His mum raised her arm and put it across Buddy's shoulder, pulling him closer, "You can say whatever you've got to say in front of him, or not at all."

King sighed, then slid his glasses down his nose and peered over the top of them. His mum's arm had pulled his shirt tight across his neck and Buddy could feel his blood pulsing against the collar. Did King know that he had tried to get him caught by the police?

"How's Terry?" King asked, looking down at his feet.

When no reply came, he held out his hands as if in defeat.

"Carol, this isn't easy for me. Things went wrong, that's all. It was Terry's bad luck. It could've happened to anyone. Another five minutes and I'd have got done too."

Buddy's heart was beating so fiercely now that he was sure his mum must have felt it but she didn't show any sign. She merely leaned back slightly against the sink and said, "You're not the type to get caught, Des."

It sounded like a terrible insult and Buddy could see that King knew it. He sighed again, shook his head, and his fat cheeks wobbled.

"All right," he said, reaching into his coat pocket. "I know how you feel. But Terry did me a big favour, not grassing to the cops, and I owe it to him to make sure you're looked after."

He pulled a large white envelope from his pocket and dropped it on to the table. His mum stiffened, lifted her arm off his shoulder, and walked quickly to the table. She picked up the envelope and pulled out a huge wad of £50 notes.

She fumbled the notes back into the envelope and held it out to King. "We don't want your blood money."

"Carol . . ."

"Take it!"

They stood looking at each other for a moment then King slowly reached out and took the envelope and put it back in his pocket. "Have it your way," he said, "but if you ever need anything . . ."

"You'll be the last to know," his mum said, and turned her back on him.

King raised his eyebrows, then shrugged and walked out of the door. Buddy waited a few seconds then went to the window. King was hurrying away down the street.

"Make a cup of tea for us, will you, love," his mum said, going back to the sink as if nothing had happened.

Buddy made the tea then went back outside and got on with the painting. How much money had there been in the envelope? There must have been at least fifty notes and if they'd all been fifties that meant – two and a half grand. His mum's job paid quite well but they weren't exactly rolling in money. Two and a half grand! He could've bought a radio-cassette player. His mum could have bought new clothes. They could have spent money on the house – all sorts of things. He knew why she'd turned it down, but the more he thought about it, the more sure he was that he would have taken it. After all, refusing it wouldn't get his dad out of prison.

There was no point in trying to persuade her about the money, but he did want to talk to her about King's visit and later that evening he asked her if she'd been scared.

"What, of that little creep? Of course not."

"Dad is."

"Yes, well, your dad's just weak."

It was like being hit, and Buddy shifted uncomfortably in his chair and pulled at the cushion, pretending he wanted it in a different place. He had thought all sorts of bad things about his dad in his time but he hated to hear his mum say anything slightly critical. Was it true that his dad was weak? And did it mean that his mum didn't love him properly? There was a long silence and he wished he could just get up and leave but there was something else he had to clear up. He counted to ten and then asked.

"Do you think King knows I told the police?"

His mum looked up from her magazine as if she couldn't believe the question.

"Don't be daft. Don't you think your dad made sure you were kept out of it?"

"You said he was weak." It came out fast and a bit spiteful because he'd been hurt by what she'd said.

"He is – with Des King. But he'd die rather than let anything happen to you. Don't you realize that?"

He nodded and started pushing the cushion again so that he didn't have to look at her. There was another silence. He forced himself to stay for a few minutes then he said goodnight and went to bed.

On Monday another visiting order came and he knew that this time he would have to go through with it.

3

His mum kept looking across at him while they were sitting on the train and he knew she was wondering if he was going to break down again. He wanted to tell her not to worry, but he didn't know how to say it.

"What's up?" he finally asked as he caught her looking again.

"Nothing. What do you mean?"

"I'm all right," he said.

"I never said you weren't."

She turned and stared out of the window and didn't look at him again until the train pulled in at Atterbury.

All the way up the hill to the prison he kept telling himself it was just like going to the dentist – you made up your mind and went in and sat there and let it happen. It wasn't going to last for ever, and it wasn't going to kill you.

As they stopped at the crossing opposite the main gates and he pushed the button for the lights, Buddy saw a large red post office van come round the bend. A mad thought flashed across his mind – if the lights changed before the van went past, everything would be all right. He wished he'd never thought it, but it was too late: he had to play the game.

There was a lot of traffic and it was moving slowly so there was a good chance that the lights would change in time, but he pressed hard on the button again. Watching anxiously, he saw the van draw nearer. He stabbed his finger on the button and kept it there. In a few seconds it would be too late. Buddy clenched his teeth and willed the traffic to stop. Car after car passed and the van was nearly there. Then a yellow car braked and the traffic drew up behind it. The post office van was four cars back in the queue – plenty of room to spare. It was a good sign.

Two old ladies were waiting at the gate and the small door opened as soon as Buddy and his mum got there. They all went through and up the steps into the office. Buddy couldn't take his eyes off the two ladies – the way they walked, the way they joked and laughed with the prison officer behind the glass made it seem as if they were just out for a good afternoon of fun. It seemed wrong – how could they be so happy when they were going to visit someone in prison?

He was so busy watching the old ladies that he hardly noticed his mum hand in the visiting order and get it stamped. The next minute they were out in the passage, walking towards the iron-bar gates. The two ladies ahead of them were still laughing and talking loudly. The iron gates swung open and they all walked through to the courtyard.

"All right?" his mum asked. She slipped her arm through his and smiled at him. "Don't say anything to your dad about Des King. It'll only upset him."

He nodded, then fixed his eyes on the white sign that hung on the swing doors of the building ahead of them – Visiting Room. This was it. A few more steps and he would see his dad.

The room was smoky, noisy and full of people sitting at tables. The two ladies immediately waved to a fat man and went over to sit with him but Buddy couldn't see his dad anywhere.

"Let's grab a table," his mum said and they sat at one in the middle of the room.

She opened her bag, pulled out a mirror and quickly checked her make-up and hair. There was a counter at the far end of the room with a queue of people waiting to buy drinks. The whole place was just like a café except for two prison officers standing against one wall. Their eyes flicked quickly round the room, probably checking that no one was trying to hand anything over because there was a big notice on the wall saying that it was forbidden to give things to prisoners.

There was still no sign of his dad. Had he decided not to come, as a kind of revenge for what had happened last time? A couple of tables away the two ladies who, a few minutes ago had been full of laughter, were now holding the fat prisoner's hands. The man was talking quietly and the ladies were both leaning towards him, peering intently at his face. Their eyes were red-rimmed and there were tears pouring down their cheeks.

Buddy felt his mum move suddenly and when he looked up he saw his dad standing in the doorway. He was dressed like the other prisoners – blue denim trousers, a faded blue shirt and a grey V-necked jumper. He seemed smaller somehow, but his face lit up with a smile when he saw them and it was the same big, cheerful smile Buddy knew so well. It was the same bouncy walk, too, as he made his way towards them. And it was the same voice.

"'Allo, love," he said, kissing his mum on the cheek. Then he turned to Buddy, ruffled his hair, tweaked his nose, and tapped him under the chin – the same greeting he always gave him. "'Allo, mate. 'Ow you keeping?"

Buddy smiled and shrugged.

"I'll get some tea," his mum said and walked off to join the queue.

Buddy and his dad sat down.

"You made it this time, then," his dad said with a grin.

"Yeah. I'm sorry about last time."

"Look – I don't want to hear no sorries about nuffin'. Nuffin', OK?"

Buddy nodded.

"Good. School all right, then?"

"Yeah, OK."

His dad smiled, but suddenly glanced at the queue and leaned closer towards Buddy.

"Your mum OK, is she?"

"'Course she is. Why?"

"Goes out, does she?"

"A bit. She goes to see her friend Joyce. We went to the pictures . . ."

His dad put his hands flat on the table with his thumbs touching each other and began tapping with his fingers, lost in thought. His face had become serious and Buddy noticed how pale he was. His fingers continued to tap on the table for a while then he clenched his fists and stared at them.

"Buddy," he said softly, "if she starts seeing some other geezer you'll tell me, won't you?"

"She wouldn't."

"You never know. It's hard for her, being on her own. I wouldn't stop her but . . . I'd 'ate it if it was going on and I didn't know. Promise you'd tell me."

Buddy nodded and glanced over his shoulder. His mum was at the counter now, putting the tea on a tray. She walked to the cashier then looked towards them and smiled.

"She wouldn't," he said, turning back to his dad.

"Yeah, well . . . You get a lot of time to think about it in 'ere."

A moment later, his mum came back with the tea and sat down. His dad became all smiles again and started joking about, saying how some prisoners never drank tea because they reckoned it was spiked with tranquillisers to keep them quiet.

His mum was just about to take a sip of hers but she suddenly lowered it and said, all serious, "It's not, is it?"

His dad roared with laughter and from then on there was no stopping him. He told them all about life in the prison and he managed to make everything sound funny and interesting. They heard about Harry, the man who shared the cell with him, and how he snored all night, and how for the first week his dad kept waking up and thinking that there was a pig in the room, but how he'd got used to it now. And how lucky it was that Harry liked Rock 'n' Roll, too, and how they listened to his cassettes all the time and talked about the music.

"When I close my eyes and listen to them songs," he said, "it's like I ain't in nick at all. It's great, the music."

For a moment his eyes looked sad but the next second he went racing on with a funny story about a prisoner who'd bought some extra tobacco. The warders had made a sudden search of the cells and the man had dropped his tobacco into his tea to hide it, then had to spend hours trying to dry it out.

"'Ere," he said, turning to Buddy. "I've given up. Mug's game, smoking. Everybody in 'ere puffs themselves to death all day. Mind you, I miss it like mad. You 'aven't started, 'ave you?"

Buddy shook his head.

"Well, don't. And don't go messing round with drugs neither. There's a lot of that stuff in 'ere, too. Some geezers'd sell their grannies to get 'old of it. I'll knock your block off if you start that lark. 'Ere, the chaplain came round the other day . . ."

And he was off on another funny story. Joke after joke and laugh after laugh, but all the time he was laughing Buddy kept looking at his dad and thinking about what he'd said about having lots of time to worry about his mum. He was making it all sound funny but if he told the same stories with a sad voice it would all sound sad and awful. And the nearer the time they would have to go, the faster his dad talked. He and his mum couldn't get a word in edgeways. They just sat and smiled and laughed. Then, when the visiting time was over, his dad stood up suddenly and said, "Oh well, got to go. See you."

Before they even had time to say goodbye, he was walking away. He didn't stop and wave, just walked through the swing doors and disappeared.

They sat staring at the doors. Then his mum picked up the cups and put them on the tray. She took out a tissue from her bag and wiped the table where his dad had spilled some tea. Getting up, they walked to the door.

"I'd rather he just sat there and cried," his mum said as they stepped on to the pavement and the prison doors slammed behind them.

4

Buddy's end of term exams came at the same time as his mum's exams and during the last week they sat together every evening, revising and testing each other. He didn't really feel nervous about his exams but he pretended he was because he could see how worried his mum was.

"I don't know what you've got to worry about," she said as they both got ready to leave on the first morning of the exams. "You're not a dummy like me."

"You're not a dummy."

"Yeah, well, we'll see, won't we."

All day he wondered how she was getting on but as soon as he got home he knew everything was all right. She was sitting on the front doorstep in the sun, drinking a cup of tea and looking at the exam paper. When she saw him she broke into a big grin and waved the paper in the air.

"It was easy," she called.

"There you are – I told you," he said as he sat down beside her. She put her arm round his shoulder and gave him a big squeeze, kissing him on the cheek. He was so glad to see her happy that he didn't mind that she didn't bother to ask how he'd got on.

Every day for the next week and a half there was the same happy grin when he got home. Even after the exams finished she was still full of it and when they went to the prison for a visit she talked almost non-stop about what questions there had been and how she had answered them. Buddy knew that this dad didn't really understand what she was going on about but he seemed pleased and kept saying, "Great!" Then, suddenly, near the end of the visit, he slumped down in his chair and said, "OK, OK, that's enough."

His mum stopped, surprised. "What's the matter?"

"Make me feel a right idiot, you do."

"Oh come on, Terry. Don't be silly."

"I'm not silly," he snapped back. "'Ere you, I ain't silly – right?"

"I didn't mean . . ."

"Yeah, I know what you mean."

"Terry . . ."

"Just leave it out!"

Buddy looked down at the floor and started to kick an old cigarette butt around with his foot. There was a long long silence but he didn't dare speak in case his dad got angry again. Finally, he lifted his arm slightly and glanced at his watch. There was a violent shake of the table and the scrape of a chair leg on the floor.

"Don't worry," his dad said. "I'm just going."

Before he could say a word, his dad had walked away fast, pushing past the other tables and then out of the swing doors.

Buddy had got into the habit of writing to his dad twice a week. He tried to make the letters as long as possible because he hoped they gave his dad pleasure and filled up some of the long hours, so he normally put down almost everything that happened to him. When his exam results came out, though, he didn't know what to do. If he wrote about how well he'd done, he might upset his dad again. On the other hand he wanted to tell him that he was one of only three people in the class who had been chosen to take all their exams in the fourth year. It was good news and it might cheer his dad up. In the end he spent ages writing about some of the mad things people had done on the last day of term and then, underneath 'Love Buddy' he wrote, 'P.S. I think I've done OK this year.'

The other thing he didn't tell his dad about was the message he'd found written on his desk in the last maths lesson of the term. He saw it as soon as he sat down. The ink was still wet so it must have been written during break just before he'd come in. It read 'Debbie + Buddy = Love'.

There was only one Debbie in his class – Debbie Bishop – and he turned round at once but she was talking to her friend, Barbara, and didn't notice him. Had she written it or had someone put it there for a joke? All through the lesson he kept thinking about it, and when the teacher did some algebra on the board he wondered if Debbie had deliberately written it as an equation because it was the maths room. If it had been the French room would she have written 'Debbie aime Buddy'?

He turned round again and this time she looked at him briefly. There had been nothing special in the look – it could have been between any two people who happened to catch each other's eye. And now that he really thought about it, she had never given a sign that she liked him. True, she had never been one of the people who'd made him feel he didn't belong in the 'E' stream, or who had made racist jokes about his black friends, Julius and Charmian Rybeero. On the other hand, she never really seemed a part of the class at all – she was very quiet and spent all her time with her equally quiet friend, Barbara.

Yet he wanted to believe that she had written it. It made a sort of warm glow in his stomach and a couple of times he found that he couldn't stop his lips from curling into a smile. He turned to the back of his exercise book and wrote DB on the dark-grey cover. Then he added BC and drew a heart round the letters. He looked at the drawing for a while then suddenly felt stupid and inked it in until the letters were invisible and he had changed the heart into a circle.

For the rest of the day he kept daring himself to say something to her, but he didn't. And now it was the summer holidays and he wouldn't see her for over six weeks. He tried to tell himself it was all silly but it kept gliding back into his mind at odd moments, and whenever he thought about it he couldn't stop himself from smiling.

The first few days of the holiday were great. He lounged in bed until late, then got up and read or watched TV, enjoying doing nothing. But after four days he was bored. The hours dragged by and he soon got fed up with walking into town and looking at the shops because he had no money to spend. Julius and Charmian had gone down to stay with relatives in the West Country so he didn't even have any friends to go and see. He dreamed of finding something interesting to do to make the time pass more quickly.

His dad felt the same. The next time they went to see him he was pale and his face was becoming puffy and his eyes had lost their sparkle.

"It's all this doing nuffin'," he said. "It drives you round the twist."

"Don't they make you work and things?" Buddy asked, remembering all the films he'd seen where prisoners had to sew mailbags and break rocks with sledgehammers.

"Don't make me laugh. The workshops are closed 'alf the time 'cos there ain't enough screws to run 'em. I put meself down for everyfing going and I've done three days' work the whole time I bin 'ere. Me muscles are all going soft. Put meself down for the gym but there's a waiting list for that an' all. I'll be a right mess by the time I get out of 'ere, I tell you. Me body's going to pieces."

The look of anger and despair in his dad's eyes stayed in Buddy's mind and he knew he must never moan about being bored. At least he was free: he could walk out in the sun, run, polish the Harley, work – all the things that his dad would love to do.

He made up his mind to get work, and he went everywhere he could think of – shops, garages, factories, cafés – but they all told him the same story: there were more people than jobs and, anyway, he was under-age. Then, finally, he found something. The man at the big fruit and vegetable depot on the industrial estate hired him for three hours every morning to clear up after the delivery lorries had gone. It was dirty and heavy work, stacking hundreds of empty crates and picking up the rotten fruit and veg, but he didn't mind. It was something to do and though the pay was terrible it meant he didn't have to ask his mum if he wanted money.

At least the time always passed quickly. When it was hot he took off his shirt and let the sun beat down on his skin as he sweated and strained to lift the crates. His muscles ached but he felt as if he was doing it for his dad – as if making himself strong and fit would stop his dad's body from going to pieces like he'd said.

The only thing that he didn't like abut the job were the two tramps who came round every day at midday, as regularly as clockwork. They smelt awful and he felt sick when he saw them picking up the squashed tomatoes or bruised fruit from the ground and stuffing them in their mouths. Sometimes juice and seeds ran down their chins and dripped on to their clothes, but though they disgusted him he found himself forced to look. How had they got like that? Once, they had been young like him. Did it mean he could end up like them? It frightened him, the same way as it frightened him to see people in wheelchairs, or the mad people who mumbled and talked to themselves in the street. Terrible things could happen to you in life and there was no way of stopping them. It was like dying – it was going to happen. Once you were born you were bound to die and there was no escape. You could tell yourself it wouldn't happen for years and years, but you couldn't even be sure of that. One day . . .

When he got home from work he always had a bath to get rid of the dirt and, partly, to wash away all the bad thoughts that the two tramps always seemed to start in his head. Then he usually settled down to listen to music or watch TV until his mum came home.

One afternoon, he was lying on his bed wondering whether to walk into town or down to the sea, when he suddenly noticed his old guitar crammed into the gap between his chest of drawers and the wall. His dad had bought it as a present for his twelfth birthday. It was second-hand and a bit battered, and after a few days he'd broken a couple of strings and lost interest in it. He had put it in the corner and left it there ever since.

He got up, pushed the chest of drawers slightly to the side, and slid the guitar out. The two broken strings jangled against the other strings as he wiped the dust off the wood. He sat down on the bed and twanged the bass string, then ran his finger up the fretboard for a few minutes listening to the different notes. Buddy stood up and walked into his mum's bedroom.

There was a mirror on the inside of her wardrobe and he opened the door and stepped back to look at himself. He swung the guitar up into position and pretended to play it while he hummed a song. His face had caught the sun during the days that he'd been working and when he smiled at himself his teeth flashed white against his brown skin.

"And here he is," he said out loud, "with this week's number one. Buddy Clark!"

He crashed his thumb up and down on the old strings and started singing a Buddy Holly song called 'Rave On'. He didn't know any chords and the guitar was all out of tune but he kept on singing, pounding the strings to the beat. At the end he bowed to the imaginary applause. As he stood up, he found himself looking into his dad's eyes in the mirror. They were reflected from the big photo that his mum kept on her bedside table and they seemed to be smiling at him.

He went back to his bedroom and put the guitar down, but not into its old position in the corner. He left it standing against the wall next to his bed, ready to be played.

5

When he got his first week's wages Buddy went into town and bought a new set of strings for the guitar. He also looked through the rack of music books and chose a book of chords and a collection of Buddy Holly songs. The man in the shop told him that he would need a pitch-pipe to help him tune the guitar so he bought one of those, too, then rushed home to get started.

It took him ages to put the strings on, and even longer to tune the guitar, but at last it was ready. He opened the Buddy Holly songbook and found a song that didn't have many chords. It was 'Crying, Waiting, Hoping'. As he looked at the words he couldn't help remembering how his dad used to play the record when his mum had left home and gone to live with her friend, Joyce. At that time the words had seemed to fit the situation perfectly:

'I'm crying, waiting, hoping
You'll come back,
You're the one I love
And I think about you all the time.'

But now, of course, they fitted what he felt about his dad being in prison.

The first chord was G and he looked in the book to see how to play it. The diagram showed that one finger went on the thinnest string and two other fingers went on the two thickest strings. He put his hand round the neck of the guitar and tried to place his fingers on the right strings. The first one was easy on its own but it kept slipping off when he reached across to put the other two on. He tried for about ten minutes and then gave up because his fingers ached. It was ridiculous. Watching people playing on TV it looked dead easy, and they moved their fingers really fast. Perhaps there was something wrong with his hands. He flexed his fingers and had another go but it was no good, so he tried the second chord instead. When he found this one just as hard, he gave up altogether and spent the rest of the afternoon standing in front of the mirror singing along to records and pretending to play the guitar.

It was good fun and he liked to see himself holding the guitar but it nagged him that he couldn't play it. So, after the meal, he went up to his room and tried again. At first it was just as hard, but he kept working at it and by the end of the evening he found that he could play the two chords quite well. He was a bit slow moving from one chord to the other and sometimes his fingers got tangled up, but he went down to show his mum.

He played 'Crying, Waiting, Hoping' and though he had to stop strumming the guitar whenever it was time for the third chord he got through it without a mistake. His mum thought it was really good and asked him to sing it again, but this time he made a lot of mistakes and it sounded terrible.

"Never mind," she said, "you've got ever such a nice voice. Your dad would be well pleased if he could hear you. It sounded just like Buddy Holly on some bits."

The tips of his fingers were very sore the next day and they had deep red marks on them from pressing on the strings but he was determined to learn how to play the third chord. After a while his fingers became almost numb, but by the time his mum got back from work he could play all the chords for the song. She

* Words of "Crying Waiting Hoping" by Buddy Holly used by permission of Southern Music Publishing C. Ltd., London.

said he'd made terrific progress and, later in the evening, they sang the song together a couple of times with her doing the harmony bits.

From then on he practised every day, and after two weeks he had learned twelve chords and could play most of the songs in the book. He loved it and even when he was at work he often made chord shapes on the handle of the broom while he was sweeping up, and whenever he listened to music he tried to work out what chords were being used.

The only thing that seemed as interesting as the guitar was Debbie Bishop. He often thought of her and one day, on his way back from work, he saw her walking towards him along the street. She smiled and stopped to ask if he was having a good holiday. He told her about learning the guitar and she seemed quite interested but, before he could pluck up the courage to mention the writing on the desk, she said goodbye and walked on.

He spent a long time going over the meeting in his mind. They'd never met out of school before and she'd looked much prettier in that pink T-shirt than she did in school uniform. If only he'd mentioned the message. Still, he promised himself, next term he'd force himself to say something.

Most of the songs he knew were about love, and whenever he sang them now they weren't just about any old girl, they were about Debbie. He even tried writing a song for her. It was called 'Love Dreaming' and though he couldn't ever get the verses right he really liked the chorus.

'Spend my whole life scheming
I'm always seeming
To be dreaming
Love dreaming of you.'

He sang it over and over and thought of Debbie. He imagined holding her, kissing her. He imagined what his mum and dad would say when he brought her home and told them he loved her. He imagined what other people in his class would say when they found out, and he thought about how good it would be to send Christmas cards signed, 'Buddy and Debbie'.

Then, suddenly, all his dreams came to an end. He got a letter from Charmian that changed everything.

> 'Dear Buddy', she wrote. 'How are you? I'm terrible. Something awful has happened. Julius and I won't be coming back to school!! Dad's decided to sell the house and the business up there and start another taxi-firm down here with his brother. It's all fixed – they've made an offer on a house, and we've been put down for a new school and everything.
>
> Julius says he doesn't mind all that much but I'm going to miss everything up there. Especially you! I won't even have the chance to say goodbye because Mum and Dad are going to organize all the moving and Jules and I will have to stay down here. I can't tell you how miserable I feel. This place is a dump.
>
> Honestly, Buddy, I will miss you. Promise you'll write. Perhaps you can come and stay in the holidays.
>
> I'll write soon.
>
> Love, Char.
>
> P.S. Jules says did you find his message about DB? He says you'll know what he means. He's as mad as ever.'

Buddy read the letter three times to let it sink in. It was the end of everything. He was losing his only real friends, and his dreams about Debbie Bishop were just stupid – he should've known it was one of Jules' jokes. Worse than all that, though – what would happen to his dad? Mr Rybeero had said that his dad would always be able to have a job driving taxis when he got out of prison. It was the one thing that his dad was relying on. He'd said that people who went to prison always had difficulty getting a job afterwards but that he was lucky because he would have one to go to. Not any more.

It was going to be terrible having to tell him.

6

After a lot of thought, Buddy decided to write to tell his dad about the Rybeeros rather than saying it face to face during a visit. He wrote at great length about the guitar playing and how he could sing nearly all of the Buddy Holly songs because he knew it would please his dad. Then right at the end he just said that Char had told him that her family was moving to the West Country. It was stupid not to say it right out because his dad was bound to realize what it meant, but he hoped it might soften the blow.

Two days before the visit, his mum's exam results came. She had passed them with good grades and she was thrilled to bits. The following evening Joyce and a couple of other women from work came round to celebrate, bringing a bottle of champagne and two bottles of wine.

Buddy drank a glass of champagne with them before going upstairs. He played his guitar loudly to cut out the noise of laughter and talk from below. Of course he was pleased for his mum, but he didn't like the way she acted when she was with Joyce. Somehow, she became different: talking about things she didn't normally talk about and even using a voice that wasn't quite natural. Like tonight, she'd gone on about dreams and ESP and a book she'd read about something called astral projection. Her voice had become all serious and a bit like a vicar in a church. It always gave him the creeps when she spoke like that – she did it sometimes when she talked about his schoolwork.

"Oh, you're doing poetry. It's beautiful, poetry," she would say. "Charles Dickens – oh yes, he's a wonderful writer," she once said when he'd had to read *Oliver Twist* for school, even though he was sure she'd never read any books by Dickens.

She hadn't always been like that: it had all started when she'd left home and gone to live with Joyce. She'd come back different in all sorts of little ways. Most of the changes were really good – the way she dressed, the way she'd made the house look nicer with books and pictures, the fact that she was more interested in all kinds of things – but he wished she wouldn't use that phony voice. She was much brighter than his dad, and sometimes his dad could make him cringe with some of the stupid things he said, but he always sounded natural and he never tried to make himself sound important.

He went on strumming the guitar a bit longer, but he suddenly felt mean sitting alone thinking unkind things about his mum on her special evening, so he went downstairs. They'd finished the champagne and started on the wine so they were all a bit merry, and they spent most of the time telling funny stories about work. Thankfully, his mum didn't get a chance to use her 'serious' voice and Buddy really warmed to the two ladies he hadn't met before – Edie and Claire. Edie made him sit next to her and kept calling him 'pet' and she filled his glass with wine a couple of times and asked him about playing the guitar.

The only bad moment came as they were getting ready to go home. Joyce suddenly turned to him at the door and said, "Well, I hope your mum's shown you who's the brains in this family. Just proves what women can do when they get the chance."

Buddy knew it wasn't aimed at him, it was a dig at his dad. For some reason Joyce always needed to say something nasty about him. His face tingled with anger, but before he had a chance to say anything, Edie cut in.

"Oh, lay off the politics for one evening," she said, putting her arm round Joyce's shoulder and making a funny face at her. Joyce shrugged and the moment passed.

He helped his mum clear up and then sat for a while with her and listened to music. When his dad was there, the house was filled with the sound of rock 'n' roll records but his mum never played those. She had started listening to classical music. Buddy didn't mind it – some of the tunes were quite nice – but tonight he didn't listen to it properly and it seemed like a row. All the time he was trying to pluck up the nerve to say something to her. At last he counted to ten and forced himself to speak.

"Mum, you won't go on about your exams tomorrow, will you?"

"What d'you mean?"

"I don't know – you know what dad's like."

"That's typical, that is. You mean shut up about what I've done so I don't hurt his pride – that's what you mean."

"No, I don't. It's just – you know – after the job and everything . . ."

"That's lovely – tiptoe round the boss, make him feel he's the only one that matters. I worked hard for those exams, and now I'm supposed to keep quiet about them in case he gets upset. And what about you? I suppose you won't tell him how well you've done at school, either?"

Buddy shook his head. The record came to an end, and he watched as the arm lifted and swung back on to its rest. His mum came across as if she were going to take the record off but she squatted down in front of him. She put her hands on his knees to steady herself and smiled.

"Buddy, you ought to be proud of what you've done, not try to hide it."

"I'm not hiding it. It's just . . . "

"What?"

"Well, how would you like to be locked in there? It must be awful."

"Of course it is. But whose fault is that?"

His heart gave an enormous lurch and, before he could stop himself, he said, "Mine. It's my fault."

Her eyes opened wide and then, quickly, she hit him hard across the face. Even before the pain began to burn in his cheek and the tears filled his eyes, she leaned close and said in a harsh whisper, "It's not your fault – it's his. Stop protecting him. He's the one who got himself in this mess and he's the one who's got to live with it – not us. I mean it. Buddy, are you listening?"

He had put both hands over his face so she wouldn't see the tears but now she grabbed them and pulled them down and squeezed them tight.

"It was him, not you. Do you hear me?"

She let go of his hands and went back to the sofa and sank down. She put her elbow on the arm of the sofa and covered her eyes. He sat for a few moments listening to the low buzz from the stereo and feeling the sting fade from his cheek, then he stood up and walked to the door. She lifted her head and looked at him.

"Don't ever hit me again," he said quietly. She bit her lip and shook her head.

Ten minutes later he was lying in bed when the door opened and his mum came in.

"I'm sorry I hit you. I didn't mean it . . ."

"OK," he said, trying not to sound sulky or angry.

"Don't worry about tomorrow – I won't say anything."

She went out and he turned over to go to sleep, but his mind was racing too fast. He'd got what he wanted but it had been a horrible scene and perhaps she was right that they shouldn't hide the news. On the other hand, if they wrote it in a letter it would seem less important and the visit wouldn't be ruined.

As it turned out, the visit was worse than he could have imagined. His mum kept her word about not mentioning the exams but it came up anyway, and it was his dad who started it. The mood was gloomy and tense from the beginning. His dad was paler than ever and there were dark rings round his eyes. As soon as they sat down he brought up the job.

"So", he said, "Malcolm Rybeero's going, then?"

Buddy nodded.

"Bang goes my job."

He took some tobacco out of his pocket and rolled a cigarette.

"I've started again – as good a way of topping yourself as any other." He laughed quickly and lit the cigarette. "Better than cutting your wrists wiv a broken plate. Bloke in 'ere tried that the other day. Didn't do 'im any good. They found 'im, sewed 'im up, and shoved 'im in solitary."

He laughed again and there was a long awkward silence. Buddy tried to break the mood by talking about other things and his dad did smile a couple of times when he mentioned some of the songs he'd learned, but he didn't ask any questions or follow things up and soon Buddy couldn't think of any more to say.

There was another silence. They all looked round the room at the other tables where everybody seemed to have so much to talk about, then back at each other.

"Hey," Buddy said, "if I can earn enough money I'm going to buy a cassette recorder so I can record myself playing the guitar. Maybe I could get a job in the evenings after school."

"Oh no, you don't," his dad cut in. "I don't want you messing up your school work for a bit of money. 'Ow's he getting on, Carol?"

Buddy felt the tension rise and he glanced at his mum. She was twirling her cup in the saucer and she didn't look up as she said, "Fine."

"What's that mean?" his dad's voice was edgy and irritated. "What's up wiv you? You're in a right mood, you are."

"It means, fine," his mum said, pushing the cup away and staring at him with a flash of defiance. "It means he's going to take his exams next year. It means he's doing really well and he's too damned scared to tell you because you're so busy feeling sorry for yourself. And, incidentally, I passed my exams – all of them. Thanks for asking."

"Yeah, well, I don't know why you two geniuses waste your time coming to see someone like me," his dad said, getting up.

Buddy thought he was going to walk out again but he hesitated a moment, then went to the counter and bought a box of matches. He looked tired and old as he walked back and sat down.

"I don't know what's up wiv me," he said. "This place is sending me nuts."

The time passed terribly slowly but they all made an effort to talk even if it was only about the weather or how many people there were in the room. Then, at last, the visit was over.

Buddy took a deep breath of fresh air as they got out into the courtyard, but his dad headed away as if he wasn't even going to say goodbye. Then, after a couple of steps, he came back. He kissed his mum on the cheek and ruffled Buddy's hair.

"I don't know if I can stick this," he said.

"Don't say that, Terry. It's not for ever."

His dad closed his eyes and breathed deeply through his nose then shrugged and walked away fast.

When they got home his mum sat on the stairs and started to cry silently. Buddy sat next to her and pulled her close and held her until she stopped.

A week later, a letter came from the prison. His dad had been in a fight with another prisoner. His visiting privileges had been withdrawn for two months.

7

Buddy was glad to get back to school. The job at the warehouse had become boring and the afternoons had dragged by, especially as his mum was working longer and longer hours. She'd been promoted because of her exams and was now a personal assistant to one of the directors. She said that it was still mainly secretarial work but that it was a step in the right direction. All Buddy knew was that it meant that he spent more and more time on his own with more time to think. And recently his thoughts had been so gloomy.

He couldn't forget how bitter and sad his dad had been the last time they'd seen him, and how he'd talked about the man who'd tried to kill himself. Supposing he got so depressed without visits that he tried to commit suicide, too. The idea of death haunted Buddy. He only had to read an article in a newspaper about a disease and for days afterwards he was sure that he'd got the symptoms and that he was going to die.

Then, to make it worse, Mr Vinnel over the road did die, suddenly, of a heart attack. He wasn't very old, and when Buddy heard the news he was terribly shocked. Sometimes he spent ages looking out of the window and thinking about how he'd never see Mr Vinnel come out of his house again to take his dog for a walk. Some time later he passed Mrs Vinnel in the town and he deliberately looked away and pretended he hadn't seen her. He didn't know what to say to her and, even though he knew it was stupid, he didn't want to be near her – as if death was something you could catch.

At least when he went back to school he had other things to think about. All the teachers kept on about working hard and setting loads of homework and, on top of that, he had extra lessons after school with the other people who would be taking the exams early.

It was strange to go into the classroom every day and not see Jules and Charmian. He missed Jules being stupid, and he would have liked to be able to talk things over with Char. She was almost the only person he'd ever been able to tell things to and it wasn't the same writing them in a letter, though he tried to make sure that he sent one every fortnight. Already her letters were filled with details about people she'd met and it was obvious she was settling down quickly. She even mentioned some boy she'd met. Buddy felt sure that soon their letters would become less and less regular and that eventually they'd stop writing altogether. It made him feel sad to realize how things changed.

The other letters he got, of course, were from his dad. Usually he wrote two a week – one to Buddy and the other to his mum, though they always read them to each other. Then, in mid-October, a letter came for his mum. He expected her to read it at teatime as usual and when she didn't he asked if anything was the matter.

"Of course not," she said, then started clearing up as if she didn't want to talk about it.

A few days later he was in his bedroom, practising bar-chords and trying to work out how to use them for the Elvis song 'I Want To Be Free', when his mum came in.

She sat on the end of the bed watching him for a while.

"By the way," she said, "your dad's asked me to get rid of the Harley."

His hand froze in the middle of the song. "Why?"

She shrugged. "He thinks it's stupid to have the bike hanging around getting rusty."

"It's not getting rusty – I polish it and oil it all the time."

"You know what I mean. It's a waste just sitting out in the shed. Anyway, he's told me to sell it and that's that."

"But what about when he gets out?"

"He'll get another one, I expect – or a car. Anyway, we'll see about that when the times comes."

The following Saturday, the man arrived from the bike shop and Buddy had to take him round to the shed to show him where the Harley was kept.

"It's a beauty," the man said as Buddy pulled the cover off. "It's not yours, is it, Son?"

"No, it's my dad's," Buddy said, running his finger along the gleaming chrome of the handlebars.

"I was gonna say . . . bit big for you. Big and beautiful. Can't understand how your dad can part with it."

"He's away a lot and doesn't use it much at the moment," Buddy said.

"Well, it won't hang around for long in the showroom, this one won't – I can tell you. Hold the door open, will you? I'll run it out."

Buddy touched the seat of the Harley quickly then closed his eyes as he held the door open and let the man wheel it away. He went straight upstairs and lay on the bed, not wanting to watch it being loaded on to the trailer. A couple of minutes later he heard the man come in and talk to his mum for a while. Then the front door slammed. The truck's engine roared and it started off. At the last moment Buddy sprang off the bed and looked out of the window. He caught a fleeting glimpse of the back wheel of the Harley as the van disappeared round the corner. It wasn't just a bike that had gone – it was memories, and a part of his dad.

When October came to an end, Buddy turned the page of the calendar to November and looked at the two days he had marked with big red rings. The first one was his fifteenth birthday, and the second was the date when his dad's visits were due to start again. He wouldn't be there to celebrate his birthday but it would be great to see him a couple of days later. He just prayed that he wouldn't do anything stupid in the meantime and lose his privileges again.

The morning of his birthday his mum told him that she would be working a bit late but that she would bring some food home with her.

"What do you fancy?" she asked.

"Scampi and chips."

"OK. And I'll get some cider or something. We'll have a special meal and I'll give you your presents."

There were six letters for him lying on the mat when he got home from school. He recognized the writing on four of them – his dad, his mum, Char, and his aunt in Bridlington. He hadn't seen his mum's sister for years, but she never forgot his birthday. The other two, though, were a mystery. He went upstairs and forced himself to get changed before he opened them because the waiting made it more of a thrill.

He sat on his bed and started with his dad's. It wasn't a card, it was a piece of prison notepaper. He had drawn a guitar and underneath he had written 'Happy Birthday. See you soon. Love, Dad.' Buddy smoothed out the crease in the middle then folded it so the prison address at the top wasn't visible and pinned it on the wall next to his bed.

He was itching to find out who the unknown letters were from but he deliberately opened the ones from his mum, his aunt and the twins. The one from the twins had a picture of a smiling old man in a deck-chair and the words 'Happy Birthday to a lovely Grandad'. Inside, Char had written, 'Guess who chose this card! Miss you. Love and kisses, Char.' Julius had added, 'Don't miss you. How does it feel to be an old man. Fancy being past it without ever having it! Kisses, cuddles and a kick in the teeth, Jules.'

Now, at last, he allowed himself to open the other two. The first one was from Joyce and he put it straight back into the envelope because he didn't really like her and he couldn't help feeling that she'd only sent it to please his mum. He picked up the last envelope. The card had a picture of an old-fashioned car on the front. Inside, there was a folded twenty-pound note and the words, 'Your Dad told me it was your birthday. Have a good time – Uncle Des.'

A shock tingled up Buddy's spine. Des King. Almost before he knew what he was doing he had torn up the card and the envelope and was on his way downstairs. He grabbed a box of matches from the kitchen and went into the back garden. At the far end of the garden, where they sometimes lit bonfires, he put the pieces of card on the small heap of old ashes and lit them. Only when they were completely burnt, and there was no chance of his mum ever finding out, did he go back inside.

The twenty-pound note was lying on the floor and he picked it up and put it in his pocket. His mum would have burned that, too – and perhaps she would have been right – but twenty pounds would always come in useful, even if it did come from someone he didn't like. Anyway, it was King's way of saying sorry about his dad. If only he knew what Buddy had tried to do to him. . .

The whole thing was disturbing, though. Buddy was sure that his dad had stopped seeing King after his arrest, so why was he back in contact with him now? Perhaps he was thinking of going back into stealing – especially now that the taxi job had gone.

Buddy was still worrying about that idea when his mum got home. He laid the table while she unwrapped the scampi and chips and poured the cider, then they sat down to eat. At the end of the meal he showed her the cards.

"Oh, isn't that nice of Joyce?" she said, going through them. "Right – time for the presents!"

She left the room and came back carrying two parcels. She put them on the table and watched as he opened the first one. It was a sweater – blue, with a pattern of darker blue and grey diamonds on the front.

"That's from me. Like it? I hope it fits."

He tried it on and told her it was perfect. Then he started on the other parcel.

"It's from your dad. I bought it, of course, but he told me exactly what to get."

Buddy pulled the paper off and opened the box. It was a large radio-casette player.

"You said you wanted one," she said as he looked up at her in astonishment.

"I did but . . ."

He had been round the shops and knew that this machine was about the most expensive there was. A terrible thought struck him. Was Des King involved in this, too. How else could there be enough money?

"Where did the money come from?" he asked.

"Well, that's nice . . . Aren't you pleased?"

"They cost a fortune, these."

"I know."

"Well? He hasn't got that sort of money."

"Oh, Buddy, use your loaf. Why do you think he sold the Harley?"

His heart clenched with a stab of pain and he pushed the box away from him. "I don't want it."

"Don't be so ungrateful. If he could see you . . ."

"But the Harley – he loved it!"

"'Course he did, but he loves you more. Don't you understand him yet? Take it. You'll break his heart if you don't."

He remembered the vow – he'd sworn never to hurt his dad. All right – if it made him happy, he'd accept the present, even though it had cost the Harley. He'd accept it. But someday, somehow, he'd make it up to him.

8

As his dad breezed in through the doors of the visiting room and saw them, his face lit up into a broad smile. It was going to be a good visit. There was a bounce in his walk and his head was held high, but most of all it was that smile – warm and open, almost cheeky. It was a smile that said, 'Let's have fun. Nothing is serious.' No matter how fed up you were with him, no matter how thoughtless or annoying he was, he only had to break into that smile and you could forgive anything.

Buddy stood up. He wanted to run and hug him tight like he used to when he was a kid – hug him so tight that it felt possible to melt away and become someone else. That smile was like a mysterious promise. Buddy only had to see it and it made his heart feel a painful longing for something, a reminder that there was somewhere better than all this.

He was here now, standing in front of him, and Buddy wanted to crush himself against him and tell him everything: his hopes and fears, how he wanted to understand things, how the selling of the Harley was one of the most generous things he'd ever known, and how he could cry just thinking about him.

Yet, here he was in front of him and all he could say was "Hello" as his dad ruffled his hair. A kind of barrier clamped down across his chest, preventing the real words and feelings from getting out. All he could do was force a mumble – "Thanks for the present."

"Do you like it?"

His dad had given him another chance to say what he really felt, but again the wave of emotions couldn't crash its way through that barrier. He couldn't even make himself look at his dad and smile. All he could do was squeeze out an insincere, "Yeah, it's great," and sit down, feeling awkward and clumsy.

It didn't matter, though. Nothing could cloud the sunniness of his dad's mood. Jokes and funny stories bubbled out of him as if he were trying to cram all the lost visits into this one. He was even optimistic about the future, talking about how he couldn't wait to start working again.

"Never know – I might start me own taxi-firm now old Malcolm Rybeero's gone. 'Course," he added teasingly, "won't really 'ave to worry now you got your new job, Carol. By the time I get out you'll be a flippin' managing director. Said you was a genius, didn't I?"

She laughed and told him not to muck about, but it was obvious she was pleased that he asked her questions about the job and said encouraging things.

The time flew past. Then, right at the end, his dad asked about the guitar playing. Again Buddy wanted to say something that would make him happy. He wanted to sound enthusiastic and say how the cassette recorder would help, but all he did was shrug and say, "It's OK."

"Blimey, ain't 'alf modest, aren't you?. Go on, Carol – tell us what 'e's like."

"He's good. He sings really nice and he's picked up the guitar ever so quick. Sounds just like the records."

His dad beamed with delight. "Cor, can't wait to 'ear it," he said, then looked round as the prison officer announced the end of the visit. "Stone me – that went quick. Oh well, see you soon. 'Bye, love."

He kissed his mum and chucked Buddy under the chin and winked. "Keep it up, eh."

Buddy nodded and, as his dad walked away, he could hardly stop himself from smiling. He had had an idea and he wanted to get home and start at once. He was going to make a cassette for his dad and send it to him for Christmas.

At first he decided not to tell anyone but after a few days he couldn't keep it bottled up any longer so he mentioned it to his mum and made her swear not to say anything about it on the next visit. She thought it was a brilliant idea and even helped him to choose the songs. He'd started to learn some of the modern songs that were in the charts but he knew that his dad wouldn't like them, so he stuck to the old songs by Elvis and Buddy Holly and the Everly Brothers.

Once they'd selected the songs he practised them every day, learning the words and the chord changes. Only when he knew them by heart did he set up the recorder and hear what they sounded like. He sang all ten of the songs, one after the other, then ran the tape back and sat down to listen. At the end of the second song he switched it off and wiped the whole tape. It sounded terrible. The guitar was plonky and much too loud, and though his voice sang all the right notes, it was lifeless and boring.

He felt like giving up the whole idea but he went downstairs and listened to the original records over and over. The more he listened, the more he realized why his dad loved them so much. They were all simple songs, but somehow the singers made them sound beautiful – sad, or full of hope and longing. They could make him feel like he'd felt when he'd seen his dad walk through the door with that smile on his face.

The following day he started again. First of all he had to get the balance of the recording right so that the guitar didn't drown everything. He spent ages experimenting – sometimes doing ridiculous things like standing in the doorway and turning the guitar towards the hall while he leaned his head into the room to sing. At last he found that he could get the correct balance if he knelt on the floor and put the recorder on his desk. That way he could sing straight into the mike, while the guitar was lower down. It felt a bit weird, but it worked. Once he'd got that right he spent a whole week concentrating on his guitar playing until the chord changes and the strumming were smoother.

Then it was time to start recording properly. He had arranged the songs so that there was a good mixture of rhythms and he had deliberately put one called 'Maybe Tomorrow' first because it was the simplest to play. He knelt on the floor in front of his desk, pressed the 'record' button, and began. Everything seemed perfect and after the final chord faded away he played the song back. The balance between his voice and the music was good and he was pleased with the guitar playing, but he was still disappointed with his singing.

He played the tape again, trying to hear what was wrong. He sang in tune, and sometimes he even sounded like the high voice on the original Everly Brothers record, but there was something missing. It was mechanical and empty – an imitation of the original, only not as good. He had to find his own way of singing it.

He opened the song book and read the words out loud. Halfway through he stopped in surprise. It was a love song to a girl, but many of the lines could have been written about what he felt for his dad. There was even a bit about two people being forced apart by others, just as they had been separated when his dad went to prison.

He threw the book aside, picked up his guitar, switched the 'record' button, and began again. One clear ringing chord and then, eyes closed, he sang the words – each one of them for his dad. They were apart now but one day soon they would be together and their unhappiness would stop – Maybe Tomorrow. He sang the way he would have liked to talk to him, and this time no barrier came down to stop the emotions from coming out. He wasn't even aware of playing the chords, yet he could hear the notes singing along with him – vibrating and jangling softly in harmony with his voice, adding their stately rhythm to his message. That was what it was – a message to his dad about how much he loved and missed him.

At the end he stopped the machine and sat for a bit, breathing deeply. Then he ran the tape back, pressed 'play' and went over to the window to listen. He pulled the curtains as the opening chord chimed, and he looked out at the dark street and over the rooftops towards the lights of the block of flats on the hill. All those people behind their windows, living their lives. He stared at the patterns of lighted squares and let the music play in the background. It was good – better than anything he'd ever done before. And, without being corny or dramatic, all the emotions he hadn't been able to say to his dad were there in his singing.

He had discovered what he had to do.

It took him another two evenings to record the rest of the songs, then he played the cassette to his mum. She thought it was great but he was already starting to hear how much better it could be with other instruments, especially drums on the fast songs. Still, it was the best he could do at the moment. He wrapped the cassette up in a parcel with a card and, on the last visit before Christmas, they left it at the prison office with his mum's present, a book about Elvis Presley's life.

His mum had arranged to spend Christmas Day at Joyce's flat. Buddy wasn't very keen on going but it was better than he expected. The meal was delicious and in the evening Edie and Claire came round and everybody was in a good mood. They listened to music, drank wine, and then played silly games that made them all laugh.

It was bitterly cold as they made their way home and a few fine snowflakes swirled in the light of the street lamps. His mum shivered and tucked her arm through his as they walked along.

"It was OK, wasn't it?" she asked.

"Yeah, it was nice."

There was hardly any traffic and the click of their footsteps on the frozen pavements echoed back from the quiet buildings.

"Nearly two o'clock," his mum said, glancing at her watch. "I wonder if your dad's asleep."

"I was just thinking about him too."

She laughed gently. "We're thinking of him – perhaps he's thinking about us."

Buddy imagined his dad lying in his cell. Yes, perhaps he was still awake, thinking of them. Perhaps he was even looking at the snowflakes falling past his cell window. It must be even more terrible to be in prison at Christmas. All he could hope was that his dad had been able to listen to the cassette and that it had made him feel a little less lonely.

9

Snow fell heavily for three days and when it stopped Buddy went out sledging on Palmer's Hill. He didn't have a sledge but he found a large plastic bag and he used that to slide down the steep slope. The snow was packed hard from all the other people who were sweeping down the hill so the plastic bag went really fast. It was hard to control and the bumps kept banging the breath out of him, but he loved the feeling of speed and it was nearly dark by the time he decided to have one last run before going home.

He was halfway down the slope when he hit a big bump and found himself swerving off to the left. He shot through a stretch of unbroken snow which sprayed up into his face, then bounced on to another smooth run. There was a shout from behind and he saw a sledge hurtling down towards him. He reached out with his left hand to push himself out of the way but it was too late – the sledge runners skimmed over his fingers.

His hands were freezing cold and numb and the pain didn't start until he got home and took his gloves off. The skin wasn't broken, but the fingers of his left hand were badly swollen. It hurt to bend them, so his mum wrapped bandages round them to help keep them straight.

That was the end of his sledging but it was also the end of his guitar-playing for a while. His right hand was not hurt, though, and he had a lot of essays and notes to do for school, so he stayed in for the next few days and worked.

He enjoyed sitting in the warm kitchen with the strange pearly light coming in through the window to remind him of the snow and the biting cold outside. He was in the mood for working and he liked the feeling of getting tasks done while his radio blasted away next to him.

Occasionally the DJs played oldies from the Fifties and he always stopped work and turned the radio up even louder. It was strange – when he saw films about the Fifties it was like seeing a replay of ancient history. The people all seemed different: sort of unreal and jerky, grey and pathetic. But the rock 'n' roll songs from that time didn't sound at all old. He was fifteen and here he was listening to the radio and hearing music that his dad also must have heard on the radio all those years ago when he was the same age.

There was still thick snow on the ground on New Year's Day when they went to the prison. The train was late getting to Atterbury, and when they arrived the prisoners were already walking across the courtyard from the cell blocks. His dad saw them and broke into a run. He was wearing work-boots and the courtyard was icy and, just like a kid, he slid the last few yards and crashed into them. He grabbed Buddy in his arms and whirled round in delight.

"That cassette was fan-tastic!" he shouted, almost slipping over in his excitement. "I never thought you was that good."

"Terry, watch what you're doing," his mum said, laughing as they bumped into her.

"Sorry, love," he said, letting go of Buddy and putting his arm round her. "I can't get over it, though. 'Ave you 'eard it? It's fabulous."

"'Course I've heard it." she said. "Look, are we going to freeze to death out here or what?"

They walked into the visiting room and made their way to a free table. They'd only just sat down when his dad leaped up again and pulled Buddy to his feet. "There's Harry – you've got to come and meet 'im. 'E shares me cell – keeps asking me to play the tape. Come on."

His dad dragged him over to a table where a fat man with dark sideburns and long, slicked-back hair was talking to a small lady wearing a red chiffon scarf over her bright blonde hair.

"Harry," his dad said, putting an arm round Buddy's shoulders, "this is my boy."

"'Ello, son," the man said, looking up with a big grin that showed he'd lost his two front teeth. "You're the singer, then. You should 'ear your dad go on about you. Drives me up the wall 'e does! Only kidding, Tel. No, seriously though – that tape of yours is terrific."

Buddy shrugged and smiled. "Thanks."

"See you, Harry," his dad said, pulling Buddy back to their table. "There you are – what did I tell you? Ain't just me. 'E reckons it's great, too."

They sat down and his dad went on and on about the tape, then suddenly stopped as he saw the bandages on Buddy's fingers.

"'Ere, what you done to your 'and?"

"Bruised it sledging."

"Blimey, it ain't busted is it?"

Buddy shook his head and told him that the bruising had nearly gone and that he would be taking the bandages off soon.

"Cor, that's a relief. 'Ere you wanna take care of them fingers now. Do them in and that's the end of your guitar playing. 'Ere maybe we oughta get 'em insured."

"Don't be daft, Terry," his mum snapped.

"I mean it – they're gold, them fingers. You 'eard that tape. 'E's gonna be a star, our son."

"Don't start filling his head up with stupid ideas. He already spends too much time on all this singing when he ought to be doing school work."

"School work," his dad sneered. "Where'd school work ever get anyone?"

"How would you know? You never did any," his mum fired back.

For an awful moment Buddy thought that there was going to be one of their terrible rows as his dad's eyes glittered in anger. Then the anger faded away and he broke into a laugh. "Dead right! I was a lazy little b. Never done nuffin'. Anyway, we'll see what 'appens, eh? 'Ere . . . I've 'ad some good news."

His mum had been glaring at the table but now she looked up as his dad laughed teasingly.

"What?" she asked.

"Went in front of the parole board a couple of days ago . . ."

He stopped, teasingly, again and his mum grabbed hold of his hand and jerked it. "And? Come on, Terry – what did they say?"

"If I'm a good boy and don't murder the Governor, I'll be out by the end of March."

"Oh, Terry!"

His mum pulled his hand closer and pressed it to her lips. Despite the smile on her face, tears sprang to her eyes and Buddy knew that if he stayed, he would start crying too.

"I'll get some tea," he said, standing up.

"It ought to be champagne," his dad laughed, "but tea'll do."

When they got home Buddy took out his new calendar and drew a thick line through January the first, then counted the number of days until the end of March. Eighty-nine. From then on, the last thing he did every night was take the calendar and cross off another date.

By the time the snow finally thawed there were fourteen thick crosses on the calendar and he was starting to get rather anxious about the mock GCSEs that were due at the end of the month. His fingers were better and he could play the guitar again, but there was so much school work that there was never much time to practise. By the time the exams were over and the results came out, the rows of crosses stretched halfway through February.

There was a period of warm, sunny weather and, for a while, it seemed as if Spring were on its way. Buddy felt lively and happy. His mum was pleased because his exam results were good, and the fine weather was a reminder that it wouldn't be long before his dad came home. On the last visit he had already started talking about how he was going to paint the house when he got out and Buddy was looking forward to helping him.

Then the wind blew cold again and it rained for days and days. His mum started to come home very late in the evenings, and she even brought work back at the weekends. She told him that it was good because it meant that she was getting more responsibility and that her boss relied on her a great deal. In fact, Buddy noticed, she talked a lot about her boss nowadays and she'd stopped calling him Mr Mandell and had started referring to him as Adrian. Buddy knew it was unfair, but for some reason he disliked Adrian Mandell without ever having met him, and he hated it whenever his mum mentioned him – especially as she kept saying how nice he was and how lucky she was to work for him.

Then, one evening she didn't get back until very late. He waited up until 11.30 but when she didn't come he went to bed. He had just crossed out the seventh of March on the calendar and switched off the light when he heard a car pull up outside. He got out of bed and went over to the window.

For over a minute the car just stood there, then the passenger door opened and the inside light clicked on as his mum got out. Buddy caught a glimpse of a man behind the steering-wheel. Then his mum slammed the door and started up the steps towards the house. He heard the front door open but he stayed watching the car. The inside light of the car came on and the man leaned forward and looked at himself in the mirror and briefly touched his hair before he reached up, switched the light off again, and started the engine. Buddy saw the car glide away from the pavement, then he leaped into bed as he heard his mum's footsteps on the stairs.

As soon as he sat down for breakfast the next morning he said, "You were late last night."

"Yes," his mum said, passing the box of cereal and smiling. "Had to finish off this big rush project we've been working on. Then Adrian took me out for a meal to celebrate, as a sort of 'thank you' for all the work I've done. Buddy, you'll never guess what."

She reached over and squeezed his arm, and he felt the blood drain from his face. What was she going to tell him?

"Adrian's given me a raise. He's that pleased with how I helped him. Isn't that great?"

"Yeah, great," he said, pulling his arm away roughly and pouring the cereal.

All day long he kept remembering what his dad had said on that first visit about telling him if he ever thought his mum was going out with another man. He had promised that he would, but first he had to be sure. It was obvious that she liked Adrian Mandell, but it wasn't as if she was trying to keep it hidden or anything, so perhaps there was nothing in it.

That evening she came home at the normal time for a change and she said that now the project was completed she wouldn't have to work late for a while. She kept her word, and a fortnight passed in which she was home on time every day and didn't mention Mandell once, so Buddy's fears drifted away.

Slowly, the crosses on the calendar got nearer the Friday when his dad was due out. Buddy's term finished on the Thursday and his mum had asked for the day off work, so they were going to Atterbury together to meet him. They spent the evening before cleaning the house to make it look tidy and welcoming and Buddy made sure that the work-shed was neat, and that all the tools were in their proper places. His dad was careless and untidy with things around the house, but he always kept the shed in perfect order and went mad if anyone didn't put the tools back where they belonged.

When he went into the kitchen afterwards, his mum had just made some tea.

"Just think," he said, looking at the third chair at the table, "tomorrow Dad'll sit there and drink a cup of tea with us."

She raised the cup to her lips and sipped the tea, then put it back in the saucer and reached for the sugar. Her hand shook as she lifted the spoon from the bowl and half the sugar fell on to the table.

"Look at me – I'm a bag of nerves," she said.

"Why? What's up?"

"I don't know. It's been a long time. Things have . . . Oh, I don't know. I'm just scared. That's all."

10

The big clock on the tower above the main prison gate ticked closer to ten-thirty. Buddy glanced at his mum and noticed that she was biting the corner of her lip. She had been very quiet on the journey and her hands had trembled slightly when she'd turned the pages of the newspaper. She was dressed nicely and her hair looked lovely – shiny, and brushed back over her ears. His dad was bound to think her pretty so he couldn't understand why she was nervous. Excited, yes – his own heart was fluttering in anticipation and happiness, but there was no need to be nervous.

At precisely ten-thirty, the small door in the gate opened and his dad stepped out. He said something to the prison officer who laughed and tapped him on the shoulder then, as the door closed, he turned and grinned at them. He took a couple of steps forward then lifted his face to the blue sky and breathed very deeply. The next moment, he was running towards them, laughing and whooping with joy. He threw his arms round both of them.

"Smell that air!" he shouted. "Fresh air, after eleven months of all that stink inside! Gawd, you don't know 'ow I've longed for this. Come on, let's get out of 'ere."

He put his arms round their shoulders and walked them towards the road. As Buddy pressed the button on the pedestrian light, a car horn started hooting loudly. He looked across the road and saw the big grey Jaguar parked next to the far pavement. The hooting stopped and the driver's window slowly opened. As the lights changed and the traffic drew up to let them cross, Des King leaned out of the window and the horn started blaring again.

"Terry!" he shouted. "Welcome back to the wicked world."

His dad laughed and was about to step off the pavement when his mum grabbed his arm and pulled him back.

"Terry, don't go."

"It's Des – he'll give us a lift."

"I don't want a lift from him."

"Don't be daft. Come on."

He took her hand and pulled her across the road, just as the lights changed and the cars revved up to go. Buddy started after them then had to step back as the cars began to roll forward. His dad opened the back door of the Jaguar but his mum shook her head and refused to get in. Buddy pressed the button and waited for the lights to change. He saw his dad say something to his mum and kiss her then, like a robot, she got into the car while he slid into the front seat next to Des King. When the lights changed Buddy ran across and climbed into the back next to his mum. She took hold of his hand and held it tight, then lay back and closed her eyes.

The car purred through the busy streets and his dad rattled on about how bright and colourful everything looked in the sunshine.

"Look at them trees," he said as they reached the edge of town and began racing through the countryside. "Blimey, I forgot 'ow beautiful it is. This is the life, eh?"

Buddy smiled and nodded, but his mum didn't even open her eyes and there was a long silence.

"What about a bit of music, Des?" his dad said at last.

"Whatever you want, Terry, my son." King switched on the radio and for the rest of the journey the music filled the car. Nobody spoke.

Buddy couldn't wait to get home. This was meant to be a happy day. Why did King have to come and spoil things?

And why did his mum have to make it worse by going all quiet and moody? He squeezed her hand, hoping she might open her eyes and cheer up, but she didn't move.

When they finally turned into their road, Buddy thought that the agony was over but he was wrong. They had barely drawn up outside the house before his dad said, "What about a drink to celebrate? The boozers'll be open by now."

"Good idea," King said.

"Right, you lot, 'ang on 'ere and I'll nip in and change. Got the key, love?"

She searched in her bag and handed over the key without a word. His dad went dashing up the stairs and into the house. King switched off the radio and Buddy counted the seconds to try and ignore the frosty silence in the car. Suddenly King coughed and turned round. He slid his glasses down the bridge of his nose and his eyes twinkled with a smile.

"Look, Carol," he said, "you've got it all wrong."

"I haven't said a word."

"I noticed." King chuckled. "Your silences could deep-freeze a turkey. But I want to tell you something. I came today because Terry's my mate and I wanted him to ride home in style. Nothing else. He doesn't owe me a thing but I owe him a lot and if there's anything I can do to help him, I will."

"Help him thieve again, that's what you mean," his mum snapped.

"By all that's holy, Carol, I swear I'd cut off my arm before I'd see Terry in trouble again. I swear it."

"You don't know what holy is," she said quietly, looking out of the window as if she didn't want to hear any more.

There was a bang from the front door of the house and his dad bounced down the steps. He had changed out of his jeans into his full Teddy Boy clothes – drain-pipe trousers, blue drape jacket with purple velvet trimming, and his blue suede shoes. He grinned down at the car in delight and, despite all the tension, Buddy felt a smile break on his own face.

"Now I know I'm really 'ome," he said as he got into the car. "Right, who's ready for a bit of living? Well it's a-one for the money, two for the show, three to get ready, now go, Des, go!"

King roared with laughter and with a scream of tyres they shot off towards the pub.

The bar was almost empty when they went in but it soon filled up. Almost everybody recognized his dad and came over to shake his hand or slap him on the back and welcome him home. Lots of them insisted on buying him drinks and before long the table was packed with pints of beer waiting to be drunk. Music blared from the jukebox and his dad talked and laughed non-stop.

They ordered steak and chips and his dad was so hungry that he had a second helping of chips before tucking into some cheese and biscuits and a trifle. The pub had emptied out by the time they had finished eating, but his dad still didn't want to go so he ordered coffee and a couple of big cigars for himself and King.

"Well, I'll have to push off in a minute," King said, reaching into his pocket and pulling out a big white envelope. "But before I do, I want you to have this."

His mum stiffened as Mr King put the envelope on the table and pushed it over to his dad.

"I offered it to Carol while you were inside," Mr King went on, "but she didn't want to know. Thinks it's dirty or something. But I want you to have it – no strings attached."

His dad's hand was reaching for it when his mum said, "Don't take it, Terry."

He hesitated for a moment then picked up the envelope and stuffed it inside his drape jacket. "Thanks, Des. I appreciate it."

His mum picked up her coat and, without a word, walked out of the pub. As the swing doors closed behind her, his dad crushed his cigar out in the ashtray and took a long swig of beer.

"Terry . . ." Mr King began, but his dad held up his hand.

"Forget it, Des. She gets funny ideas, that's all."

They stayed for another ten minutes but nobody could find much to say. Out in the bright sunlight of the car park Mr King offered them a lift but his dad said he wanted to walk. King got into the car and started the engine, then wound down the window.

"It's nice to have you back in the land of the living, Terry. If you need anything, just give me a bell. I've got this car-breakers yard now, so if you ever need work . . . Anyway, be lucky."

The Jaguar pulled out of the car park and sped off down the road. They strolled home slowly, his dad stopping to look at the flowers that were beginning to bloom in the gardens and the leaves that were unfolding on the trees.

"We must get some work done on our garden this year – it always looks a right tip. You'll give me an 'and, won't yer?"

Buddy nodded but he knew that the signs of Spring were only half the reason why his dad was walking so slowly. Things had started badly. More than anything he wanted his mum and dad to get on, and while he normally never said anything when they disagreed he felt that this time he had to try.

"Mum's worried you'll get mixed up with King again," he said.

"I know."

"She thinks he'll . . ."

"Look, you don't 'ave to spell it out."

They walked on in silence until they got to the end of their road. Stopping suddenly Buddy's dad pulled on his arm.

"Listen, I didn't ask Des to come and pick us up. And I didn't ask 'im for the money. What would you 'ave done? Tell 'im to stuff it? Would you? Buddy, I want to know."

He thought hard. What would he have done? He knew what his mum was scared about, but it was just a present.

"No strings attached," King had said. A present, a peace-offering for all that lost time in prison. And he remembered his reaction when King had first offered it all those months ago.

"I'd have taken it," he said.

"Honest?"

"Honest."

His dad wrinkled his lips up into a wry smile and there was a glisten in his blue eyes.

"Cheers," he said, and ruffled Buddy's hair. "Come on, let's go and sort it out."

His mum was sitting on the sofa in the front room. She was still wearing her coat and she didn't look up at them. His dad went over to the mantlepiece and picked up the model of a Harley-Davidson that always stood there. He examined it for a moment then put it back, walked over to the sofa and squatted down in front of her.

"Listen, love, I'm gonna say this just once and that's an end of it. I'm keeping the money – Des owes me a favour and it's 'is way of paying it back. But it don't mean nuffin'. I told you when I went in nick, I won't ever get in trouble again. All I want is for us to be 'appy – all three of us." He reached out and lifted her chin so that she had to look in his eyes. "The bad times are over, right? Come on, girl, give us a smile – a big one, like that one you gave me the first time I saw you down the pier wiv that fat friend of yours. Remember? Cor, you was a right looker – still are."

She tried to lower her chin but his dad held it firmly and winked at her.

Slowly her lips lifted in a smile.

"What a looker," his dad said. "What a looker!"

He leaned forward and kissed her and she put her arms around his neck and drew him close.

Quietly, Buddy slipped out of the room.

11

Buddy woke to find the sun streaming in through a gap in the curtains and music booming from below. He lay on his back and watched the motes of dust dancing in the shaft of sunlight. The music pounded so loudly that the bass notes rattled the window and reverberated through the floor. It was Buddy Holly, of course – 'Peggy Sue' – and he found himself thinking of the chord changes of the song. When it came to an end he rolled out of bed and dressed quickly.

His dad was in the kitchen, spreading marmalade on a thick piece of toast. His mum was out shopping.

"Tea's still 'ot," his dad said, "and there's toast under the grill. Hurry up, though – I want to 'ear you play the guitar after."

When he had finished breakfast Buddy fetched the guitar and sat down at the table while his dad poured himself another cup of tea. He suddenly felt nervous and he strummed it casually a couple of times, then spent ages getting it perfectly in tune.

"Go on, then," his dad said, leaning forward in excitement.

"What do you want to hear?"

"Anything, dummy – just get on wiv it!"

He started to play 'Raining in my Heart' because he really loved one of the chord changes and he'd been playing it a lot recently. He strummed through the chord sequence once and then started to sing. He watched his fingers closely but he didn't make any mistakes and at the end there was a huge smile on his dad's face.

"Go on, do some more," he said.

Buddy felt relaxed after the first one and he played for over half an hour while his dad listened and tapped out the rhythm of the fast tunes on the table-top.

"That's fantastic," his dad said, when he finished. "Cor, honest, Buddy, you ain't 'alf good. We'll 'ave to get you another guitar, though. That one's all clapped out. You need an electric one to play in a group."

"But I haven't got a group."

"Not yet, but we'll fix that. Can't make records wivout a group, can you?"

His dad's enthusiasm was exciting and Buddy loved to see him when he was lively like this but it was a bit mad to start talking about groups and records. His dad wouldn't listen to any objections, however.

"Gotta think positive, mate. Where would Buddy Holly've got if he hadn't thought positive, eh? When he was your age he was already singing at dances at 'is school."

"Dad, I'm not Buddy Holly."

"No, but one day you could be as famous as him. Wouldn't that be great? And I could be your manager."

Buddy could hardly believe his ears. He laughed and put the guitar down.

"Don't laugh – I mean it. Listen, look at me. What am I? I'm no one."

Buddy tried to cut in but his dad held up his hand and leaned close, his eyes wide and intense.

"Don't try and tell me different. I've 'ad eleven stinking months to think about it. I'm nobody and I'll never be anything else – not on my own. But you and me together . . . At least there's a chance. What do you reckon?"

All kinds of doubts flashed across Buddy's mind, but he remembered his vow. He had sworn that he would do anything to make his dad happy. Well, if it made him happy to think that they could get somewhere with music, then he'd try.

"OK. But what about school?"

"You'll 'ave to go on wiv that and get your exams – your mum'll do 'er nut if you don't. Besides, you ain't that good, big 'ead – still need to practise. But first off, we got to get you a guitar. Come on."

"Now?"

His dad beamed. "Yeah, now. That money's burning an 'ole in me pocket – let's go and blow some of it."

The music shop was full of people looking at instruments and playing them. Some of them were really good, especially a tall blonde girl who was trying out electric pianos, and Buddy felt embarrassed about playing in front of them. His dad insisted, though, and he made the salesman take all the guitars down one by one and plug them into an amplifier. The trouble was that Buddy didn't have the faintest idea what he was looking for so he just played a couple of chords quietly on each one then tried the next. The salesman noticed and began to give him advice about feeling the action on each one and seeing how comfortable it was to hold down the strings. In the end there were two which he liked, but he couldn't decide between them. His dad said he preferred the red one because it looked like Buddy Holly's.

"It costs more, though," Buddy pointed out.

"That don't matter. Got to 'ave the best," his dad said, then nudged the salesman's arm. "Gonna be a star, my boy is."

Buddy cringed, but the salesman smiled politely.

"Right, we'll 'ave the red one. Now, what about an amplifier?"

Buddy admitted he didn't know anything about amplifiers so the man went through each one, talking about watts and channels and output.

"Don't understand all that," his dad said when the salesman finished. "I like that red one, though – goes nice wiv the guitar. All right, is it?"

"Yes, it's an excellent model. And it's got a number of features which . . ."

"Good. Pack it up wiv the guitar and we'll be back later to pick 'em up."

A flicker of doubt passed across the man's face but it disappeared when his dad pulled out the envelope and began peeling off fifty-pound notes.

"'Ow much? Discount for cash, of course," his dad said. The salesman pulled a calculator from his pocket and spent ages pressing figures and then said the most he could possibly allow was seven per cent. His dad asked for ten, and when the man started to object, he put the money back in his pocket and said they'd try another shop. He turned to go but the salesman called him back and agreed.

"Smooth nerd," his dad said, as they left the shop. "I coulda probably got 'im to knock off fifteen per cent but I couldn't be bothered. Right, next stop – the video shop."

"What for?" Buddy asked, trying to keep up as his dad swaggered off down the road at a furious pace.

"To buy a sea-lion. I thought you was supposed to 'ave brains. What else do you buy in a video shop?"

They breezed into a large TV shop and his dad asked about videos. They went along the display and the man showed them the various models and explained what each of them could do. Buddy listened carefully and soon noticed that the man was talking directly to him. He looked round and realized why: his dad had gone over to the other side of the shop to a display of video cameras. One was plugged into a TV set and he was walking up and down in front of it, watching himself on the screen.

Buddy moved on with the salesman to see the rest of the recorders. They'd just reached the last one when his dad joined them again.

"Yeah, that one'll do," his dad said, casually waving his hand towards the one the man was showing. "Come over 'ere, though, I want to know about this stuff."

He strode over to the cameras and Buddy and the man followed.

"Stand there," his dad said, pulling Buddy in front of the camera. "Innit great? You can see yourself. Look." He pushed Buddy out of the way and leaned in close to the camera so that his face grew larger and larger until it filled the TV screen. He laughed in delight and opened his mouth wide.

"Urgh – you can see me fillings. Innit fantastic? Does it record an' all?"

"Oh yes, Sir. It takes a normal video cassette and you can play it back directly or use an ordinary video player. It's fully automatic – focus and lighting. Works off mains or a re-chargeable battery so, of course, it's portable. You can take it anywhere and record whatever you want."

"Cor, flipping miracle. 'Ere, we gotta 'ave one of these."

Buddy pulled him to one side and tried to persuade him to take some time to think about it, but his dad wasn't in the mood to listen.

"Money's for spending, innit? Can't take it wiv you," he said, breaking away and heading back to the salesman. "I'll 'ave it. And throw in some cassettes, too."

"Very well, Sir. The credit terms are most reasonable."

"Credit? What do you fink I am? I'm paying cash. Now then, 'ow much will you knock off it?"

Once again he bargained with the man and finally got a ten per cent discount. The man's eyes bulged as his dad produced the wad of fifties and counted them out. They left him packing the camera and the recorder into boxes for collection and set off across the road to the big department store opposite.

His dad had decided that he wanted to buy a present for his mum and Buddy followed as he stormed into the ladies' clothes department and began rummaging along the racks. He pulled out dresses and skirts and held them up against the lady who was serving them, but he didn't like any of them and bundled them back on to the racks.

Finally he stopped in front of a dummy that was wearing a dark blue coat and pointed. "That's the one – she'll look gorgeous in that. Wrap it up."

"What size, Sir?" the saleslady asked.

"Dunno. About your size, darling. Give us a hug and I'll see if you feel the same."

The lady laughed and said that she'd give them a size twelve and that they could change it if it didn't fit.

When they left the stop his dad told him to go to the TV store and bring the stuff out on to the pavement while he went to find a taxi. Ten minutes later the taxi arrived and his dad jumped out and they loaded the boxes into the boot. They stopped off at the music shop and picked up the guitar and amplifier. Then they headed for home.

Buddy sat back in the taxi holding the box with the guitar in it and added up what they'd spent. It came to over two thousand pounds. He could just imagine what his mum would say when she saw it all. On the other hand, they would never have had the money in the first place if it had been up to her – so she couldn't complain much.

"Dad, how much did Mr King give you?"

"Mind you own business," his dad said, then grinned and held up five fingers.

"Grand?" he whispered in astonishment.

"Yeah, but if you want anyfink else it's tough luck, 'cos the rest's going in savings."

The taxi driver helped them to unload and the boxes were piled up on the top step when his mum opened the front door. She took one glance at the boxes, fired an angry look at Buddy and his dad, and went into the living room. They hauled the stuff inside and his dad unwrapped the coat. Buddy followed him into the living room.

"We've been on a shopping spree," his dad said, holding up the coat. "Bought some essentials, but we decided to blow a bit on something for you – a sort of late present for passing your exams. Try it on."

His mum stood up reluctantly but as his dad helped her slip the coat on he whistled, and she couldn't help smiling.

"Like it?"

"It's lovely. Thanks," she said, pulling it tight and looking at herself in the mirror. "What's the other stuff?"

"Guitar for Buddy – essential for 'is music. And some video stuff for me."

"What's essential about that?"

"It's a secret. I'm planning for the future. Gotta move wiv the times, you know. Anyway, go and put somefing nice on so we can see the coat proper – looks daft wiv jeans. Me and Buddy'll make some tea."

"What plan have you got for the video, Dad?" Buddy asked as they stood in the kitchen waiting for the kettle to boil.

"Search me," his dad whispered. "Anyway, we'll 'ave a bit of fun wiv it, if nuffin' else. And it's about time we 'ad some fun round 'ere. What d'you reckon?"

His dad winked and Buddy could hardly stop himself from putting his arms round him and giving him a hug.

12

The two and a half weeks of the Easter holidays was one of the happiest times Buddy had ever known. Every morning he forced himself to do two hours' revision for his exams. He didn't like the work much but it felt good to have done it properly and have the rest of the day free. His dad always kept quiet while he was working but as soon as he finished they would have a cup of coffee together, and music would be put on full blast.

His dad was in a great mood – mucking about and making Buddy laugh all the time at his crazy jokes and stories. He was absolutely obsessed with the video camera and he filmed everything. He would spend hours trying to get close-ups of things like flies or trying to film Buddy and his mum as they moved round the house. A couple of mornings Buddy even woke to find the camera lens staring down at him with his dad telling him to get up and walk downstairs while he followed to record it.

"Give it a rest, Terry," his mum said one evening as he lay at the bottom of the stairs to video her coming down. "You filmed me when I came through the front door; you filmed me during the meal – it's a wonder you let me go to the loo on my own."

His dad laughed. "I tried to get in but you'd locked the door. 'Ere, come on you two, I want to try outside while there's a bit of light."

Out in the garden they were supposed to act a scene where a lady finds a young bloke asleep next to her dustbin but his dad kept giving them such daft instructions that they all got the giggles and it became too dark to go on. They laughed even more when they watched the cassette later.

"Blimey, look at that," his dad sniggered, when it got to the bit with his mum on the stairs. "We can see up your skirt. It's a porno video, this one. Let's run it back again."

"Don't you dare," she said, grabbing him round the neck as he reached for the rewind button. They struggled for a moment while she tickled him, then the garden scene came on.

"Let go of us – I want to watch this bit," his dad said. "Cor, look at you two giggling all the time. Right liabilities you are – 'ow am I supposed to become an ace cameraman wiv a couple of loonies like you giving me grief? I'll never get better."

He did get better, though – despite all the mucking about. By the end of the holidays he had made huge improvements and had learned how to zoom and pan and track properly. Some of the sequences he filmed looked really professional. He even started to criticize TV programmes, picking out mistakes and saying how they should have been done, but he liked the adverts and recorded some of them, watching them over and over to see how they were made. Best of all, though, he loved the videos they showed on pop programmes.

"It's a pity the music stinks," he said, "'cos the pictures are fabulous. Just imagine if they 'ad a few decent singers like Elvis – they'd really be the business."

Whenever Buddy started to practise his guitar, his dad appeared with the camera and moved round him recording. At first, it put him off to have the lens peering into his face or down at his fingers but he got used to it and learned to carry on as if it wasn't there. His dad kept nagging him to stand up and move around to make it more interesting. But Buddy said he couldn't practise properly like that so he usually got bored quickly and left him to play in peace. In some ways the electric guitar was easier to play than his old one. The neck was thinner, so it was easier to form the chords – but the whole sound was different and it was difficult to adjust to the technique. There was a lot to learn, and he spent hours trying to find out what it could do.

He and his dad had agreed that during the holidays they would do the cooking for his mum and they took it in turns to decide what they were going to have. His dad always chose easy things like fish fingers and oven chips, but Buddy tried some more complicated dishes. He found a recipe for a spicy stew which was so hot that none of them could eat it and they all had to go out for a burger, but some of the other things he made were really delicious. Everybody liked his corned-beef hash so much that he did it twice and the second time his dad ate so much that he spent an hour lying on the sofa with his jeans undone, moaning that he'd eaten too much while his mum laughed and said it served him right.

Buddy wished that the holidays could go on for ever, but school started again and, suddenly, the good times were over. The first day back, a couple of his teachers marked his holiday work and said it wasn't very good and that he'd have to make a big effort if he wanted to do well in the exams. He got home feeling low and found that his dad had had a bad day, too. He'd been looking for jobs and had been turned down for all of them.

"As soon as they ask what I've been doing lately I know I'm finished."

"Don't tell them," Buddy said.

"No point – they'd find out fast enough when they ask for references and stuff. It's 'opeless."

"No, it's not – something'll come up."

His mum said the same thing and they both tried to cheer him up during the meal by suggesting jobs he could try for. He stayed moody and quiet, though, and when they finished eating he went out to his workshed. Buddy and his mum washed up and went into the front room. She put one of her records on, turned the volume low, and started to read, while he did some school work. About an hour later the back door slammed and his dad came in. He slumped down in a chair and picked up the newspaper then looked at the record player.

"What's this crap, then?"

"Mozart. It's nice," his mum said.

"Sounds like someone's died. Let's 'ave something cheerful." He got up and moved towards the record player.

"Leave it, Terry. Buddy can't work with the rock and roll on loud. You're not the only one in this house, you know."

"'E can work upstairs, can't 'e?"

"Yeah, I'll go upstairs," Buddy said and he started to get up but his mum grabbed his arm and pulled him down again.

"Why should he?" she said. "Anyway, I'm not going upstairs – and I can't read with loud music."

"Read," his dad sneered. "That's all you do now – read. You never used to."

"Things have changed."

"You can say that again. Too many damned things 'ave changed round 'ere if you ask me."

"Well, if you don't like it, you know what you can do."

She said it quietly but his dad looked as if she had hit him. His mouth opened in surprise and a hurt look flashed across his eyes. Buddy looked down at his book.

"This is my 'ouse, you know," his dad shouted.

"Oh, is it? And who paid the rent while you were inside?"

Buddy kept his eyes fixed on the page but he could almost feel the angry looks they were giving each other in the silence that followed. Then there were footsteps, and his dad left the room. A moment later the front door slammed.

His mum sighed and started reading again but Buddy could feel her trembling. She turned a couple of pages much too fast to have read them and then, almost to herself, she said, "I won't let him treat me like dirt."

She put down the book and went upstairs. Buddy waited up until half past eleven, hoping that his dad would be back, then went to bed. He was lying there when he heard the key scrape in the front door lock, then the click of the kitchen light. He wondered whether to get up and talk to his dad but he couldn't think what he would say. He turned over and closed his eyes – at least he had come home.

Buddy was late getting up the next morning and by the time he got downstairs his mum had left for work. He gulped a bit of cereal then went into the front room to get his school bag. His dad was hunched up asleep on the sofa. He had pulled a coat over himself and still had his shoes on so it was obvious that he'd been there all night. He picked up the bag and tiptoed out of the house.

Nobody referred to the row but his dad didn't put his music on anymore and the bright happiness that had filled the house was gone. The cool mood lasted for over a week. Then their routines changed completely – his dad got a job as a cashier in an all-night petrol station. He wasn't very pleased – the hours were long: nine in the evening until seven in the morning; the pay was poor; and he hated the fact that it had been found for him by his probation officer – but at least it was a job. As he said, the next time he looked for work he wouldn't have to say he'd just come out of prison.

"Besides," he added, only half-jokingly, "it'll keep me out of your way, won't it, Carol? I'll take me cassette player and listen to me music down there."

He did just that. Sometimes Buddy wandered down to the garage in the evening when he'd finished his homework and as he walked across the forecourt he could hear the music blaring out from behind the plate-glass window of the booth where his dad sat. He enjoyed spending an hour or so there, talking and helping to collect the money. It made a break from studying.

"Don't know 'ow you stick all that school work," his dad said. "Worse than this lark, and that's saying somefing."

"Just want to make sure I pass," Buddy told him. "I don't want to have to take them again."

"Yeah, well that's the difference between you and me – you're smart and I'm thick, Brainbox. You'll never end up in a dead-end job like this."

"You're not ending up here," Buddy said, pushing his dad so that his swing-chair revolved.

"No, that's right," his dad said, smiling. "Just temporary – then you and me are heading for the top."

Buddy loved the walk home from the garage. Often, he stopped at the edge of the forecourt and, hidden in the shadows, looked back at his dad in the lighted booth. It was reassuring to see him there, locked in the square of bright light, with the rock 'n' roll drifting out, and his cheerful smile crinkling his face as he talked to a customer.

The summer evenings were warm and as he strolled through the estate, past the lighted houses and even the occasional gardener packing away his tools as night fell, Buddy felt an aching sense of belonging to the place.

Then, one Friday evening, he arrived at the garage and found his dad in an excited mood. He had just been talking to a man who had come to fill up a Daimler limousine that was being used for a wedding the next day. The man had said that couples liked the Daimler because it made them feel that their wedding day was something special that they would always remember.

"As soon as 'e said that, I realized I'm sitting on a little goldmine with that camera of mine. I mean, who wants photos of a wedding nowadays when you could 'ave a video of the whole thing? I could film the Church service and the party after – everyfing. I'm gonna put an advert in the paper tomorrow."

It certainly seemed a good idea and Buddy helped him draft the advertisement. They tried lots of versions, some of them funny and some of them clever, but in the end they decided on something simple.

'Memories of a Lifetime' was the title. 'Remember your special moments for ever with a colour-video recorded by a professional. Weddings. Christenings. Parties.'

"Can't put funerals really," his dad said and laughed, "or can we? No, better not. Now then,'ow are they gonna get in contact? Don't want to put an address – people 'ate writing letters. I know, I'll put the garage phone number and say after nine pm only. The boss'll never know."

The advert appeared the following week and Buddy made sure he was at the garage the first evening – although he didn't expect anyone to call. When the phone rang at 9.10 he almost jumped in surprise. He could hardly stop giggling as he listened to his dad when it became obvious that it was a reply to the ad. By the time he left at eleven-fifteen there had been six calls and his dad had fixed up four definite appointments. Two were for weddings the following Saturday – one in the morning and one in the afternoon. There was a children's party on the Sunday, and another wedding at the end of the month.

"You know what, mate?" his dad said as Buddy left to go home. "Don't say nuffin' to your mum, but I think we're on to a winner."

He said it calmly but when Buddy reached the edge of the forecourt and looked back, his dad waved to him then, with a huge grin of delight, he stood up and punched his arms above his head in triumph.

13

Buddy agreed to help his dad with the first two weddings. He bought the cassettes, made sure that the battery for the camera was properly charged, and on the Saturday morning checked that all the equipment was ready while his dad had a bath when he got home from the garage.

"Really ought to 'ave a car to cart this lot round," his dad said as he came downstairs. "Lucky they don't live far."

"Dad," Buddy said, looking at the full Teddy Boy outfit his dad had put on, "are you really going to wear that gear?"

"'Course I am. Looks great. Makes the whole thing special, don't it. People are daft like that – wear somefing different and they reckon you're interesting. They'll love it, you see."

He was right.

"How lovely," cooed the bride's mother when they arrived at the house. "A real Edwardian suit. So unusual. They had such style in those days. Is that real velvet on the collar?"

"What else? None of your rubbish. Now then, let's get organized. I wanna do the whole works so we'll start wiv you saying goodbye – then I'll get you coming down the stairs and going off to the church in the car. Are the bridesmaids 'ere? Good. We'll 'ave them, too."

Buddy watched in admiration and surprise as his dad took over the proceedings. He had never seen him so organized and efficient as he ordered everyone about, telling them to do this or that, walk here or there, and making them do it again if he wasn't satisfied. He seemed charged with energy as he rushed about, talking all the time and making them all laugh at his jokes, while he tried to find the best position and angle to film.

He filmed the bride and her father in the car as they drove to the church and he even told them what to say to each other. Then, when they reached the church, he sent the car off round the block so he could film them arriving. Buddy was a bit worried that his dad was controlling everything a bit too much, but they all seemed willing to do anything he said.

"See? People go nuts when they think they're gonna be on telly," his dad whispered as he got the guests to line up on the church path to welcome the bride. "It's like them berks at football matches, waving like mad every time the camera goes near them."

The vicar gave an irritated glance as his dad tiptoed behind him and leaned the camera in over his shoulder for a close-up on the couple as they took their vows, but even he was prepared to pose for a shot of him watching the signing of the register. The only awkward moments came after the service when they got outside and found a photographer waiting with his camera all set up.

"Who's that?" his dad asked the bride's father.

"Oh, we thought we'd have some still photos as well. You know – souvenirs for people who couldn't come and all that."

"Hm, waste of time," his dad mumbled and then proceeded to stand in front of the photographer and start to arrange people into groups.

The photographer was furious and asked him to stand aside so that he could take the photos.

"I am the official photographer, you know," the man said weakly as his dad turned round and moved threateningly towards him.

"Listen, mush," his dad said softly, and smiling so that nobody would guess what was going on. "I don't want to get 'ard wiv you. This is telly, right? And telly comes first. You can take your crummy snaps when I've finished. OK?"

The man blinked in surprise, then nodded frantically as his dad took another step closer. From then on he was in control again, calling the various people on to the church steps and moving them around and making them wait until he had chosen the best way to film them. Only when he had finished did he stand aside and, with a friendly grin, invite the photographer to do his work.

"Absolutely wonderful," said the bride's father as he paid at the end. "I don't suppose you could come along to the reception and film that, too, could you? We'd pay you extra, of course."

"Sorry, mate," his dad said, looking at his watch. "Got another wedding this afternoon. Should've asked earlier. Tell you what I'll do, though. I'll check this through and then for another thirty quid I'll hire you a video machine and a telly so you can watch it at the party."

The man accepted at once and wrote down the name of the hall where the reception was being held.

"That's a hundred and five quid altogether. Money for old rope," his dad laughed as they rushed home. "We'll 'ave to get a taxi to lug all this stuff round to the hall – still, much more of this and we'll be able to buy a car."

"Where are you going to get the video and telly from?" Buddy asked.

"Lend 'em ours, of course, stupid. We don't need it tonight. I told you me video stuff would be an earner, didn't I?"

While they quickly ate sandwiches for lunch, they played through some of the recording and Buddy was impressed by how well it had turned out. Somehow, in all the activity and bustle and tension, his dad had been able to record things in a way that made it seem calm and dignified. In particular, the actual marriage ceremony in the church was really beautiful and he had managed to catch all the best moments in an interesting way like a proper TV film.

"Yeah, it's a bit of all right, innit?" his dad said when Buddy told him how good it was. "I loved doing it, too. Fancy getting money for something you like doing. Beats working in the garage, eh?"

They dropped off the video and TV at the hall, then took the taxi on to the second wedding. It was a much smaller affair with fewer guests, but the people were obviously very rich and they talked in an extremely posh way. Buddy found himself automatically changing his accent slightly when he talked to them and taking care not to drop his aitches. It was something he did with the posh kids and teachers at school and he hated it about himself because it made him feel a phoney, rather like when his mum put on her 'serious' voice.

His dad, though, didn't seem to care – he just talked in his usual breezy way. The people had hired a vintage Rolls Royce for the occasion and, when he saw it, his dad nudged the bride's father in the ribs and said, "Wotta motor! Bin robbin' banks again, 'ave yer?"

Once again, his joky manner made everyone laugh and because they were relaxed he was able to get exactly what he wanted for the video. The man was so pleased with the finished cassette that he added a twenty-pound tip to the fee.

They had made two-hundred pounds in one day and his dad was so delighted that he put the advert in the paper on a regular basis. He also decided that they would have a phone installed at home and, typically, he ordered an answering machine as well. Soon, there were three or four bookings on all the Saturdays for the next couple of months and he was having to turn customers away.

The GCSE exams started the day after the half-term holiday. Apart from the weddings on the Saturday, Buddy had spent the whole time revising. He felt as if he had done enough work but, as he put away his books late on the evening before the first exam, a wave of panic and doubt hit him. Supposing he forgot everything? Supposing he failed? His brain was buzzing with all the stuff he'd learned but when he tried to remember things, he just couldn't. He was tempted to pull the books out and do some more revision but he knew it would only make it worse. Instead, he went down to the garage.

"Stop flapping like an old hen," his dad said when he told him how he felt. "Tell yer what – go 'ome and 'ave a good kip. Then tomorrow morning before you go off, play one of me records. It'll bring you luck, you see. Somefing nice and gentle to calm you down. I know: 'All I Have To Do Is Dream' by the Everlys – that'll do the trick."

Despite his dad, and despite the fact that his mum said that as long as he tried his best she didn't mind what happened, he slept badly that night. He did play the record, though, and the first exam went so well that he made sure he played it every morning before he left for school. He soon stopped being nervous and settled into the routine of the exams and although they were hard work he quite enjoyed them. One by one, he ticked off the subjects and put away the books and notes, hoping he would never have to learn all those facts again.

The time passed quickly and when he took the final exam at the beginning of July, he could hardly believe it was all over. Now all he could do was wait and hope until the results came out. The people who had taken the exams weren't expected to go back to school for the end of term but, on the day they ended, Mr Normington had invited all their parents for an interview to discuss the future. His mum was annoyed when his dad said he wouldn't be able to go. He kept insisting that he had to work, but it was only an excuse because their interview was at 6.30. He was still at home when Buddy and his mum got back afterwards.

"All right, was it?" he asked, without taking his eyes off the video he was watching.

"You should've come if you're that interested," his mum said coldly.

"Nah, can't stick schools – they give me the creeps. And that Normington's a right berk."

"He's an extremely polite and educated man; which is more than I can say for some people I know. Anyway, he says that if Buddy's results are as good as they expect they'll put him in the Sixth Form next year and let him start his 'A' levels."

"'A' levels – big deal," his dad said, getting up and switching off the TV. "I've gotta go. You coming down the garage later, mate?"

"Don't you try putting him off the idea of getting a decent education," his mum said, before Buddy could reply.

His dad picked up his jacket and slipped it on. "Now why would I want to do that? Don't you think I want our son to end up polite and educated like your darling Mr Normington?"

He gave her an ironic smile and went off to work.

Buddy was angry with both of them but if he stayed in, his mum would think she'd won, and if he went to the garage, his dad would think he'd won. In the end he went out without saying where he was going and just walked through the streets of the estate for a while. This way he could make them both lose. What was the matter with them? He was sure they loved each other but most of the time they were like two dogs who snarled every time the other moved. When he got home it was obvious that his mum wanted to ask where he'd been but he just said goodnight and went to bed.

He didn't go down to the garage for a couple of evenings, hoping that the subject would be forgotten by then, but it was the first thing his dad asked.

"Are you serious about all this 'A' level stuff?"

"I don't know. Blimey, Dad, I haven't even passed the others yet."

"But if you do?"

"Oh leave it out! I'm supposed to be on holiday. I want a rest from all that. Anyway, I'm not sixteen yet so I'll have to stay till Christmas at least. I'll make up my mind then. So just shut up about it."

There was a sulky silence between them. They didn't look at each other and it was a relief when a couple of customers came to pay for petrol. The silence went on and on. The booth was small and it was uncomfortable to be so close to someone and not talk because of a bad mood. He was just about to mumble goodbye and go, when his dad spoke.

"Aren't you interested in the music anymore, then?"

"'Course I am."

The silence had been broken but it felt as if it could start all over again so he forced himself to say something more positive. "I love it. I'm gonna spend the whole holiday playing."

His dad grinned and pulled a piece of paper out of his pocket. "That's all right, then – 'cos I've sent this off to four music papers and put it up on the noticeboard of the music shop."

Buddy unfolded the paper and read it.

> *'A chance for stardom. Great group (lead guitar, bass, drums) needed to back brilliant young singer/guitarist. Ring 02795836.'*

"Dad, you shouldn't have put 'brilliant'."

"Why not? You are. And even if you wasn't, you gotta think positive. If you think you're brilliant, you will be. Anyway, this way we won't get no rubbish players. Only the best for your group, eh?"

Buddy looked at the paper again. It was good fun playing the guitar on his own, but the idea of singing with a group sent a shiver of excitement running down his back.

14

The ads came out in the music papers the following week and that word ‘brilliant’ looked even worse in print. Buddy could just imagine the disappointed looks on people’s faces when they actually heard him sing. As it happened, he needn’t have worried. Although there were phone calls every day asking about the Wedding Video advert, they didn’t have a single reply to the ad about the group.

Then his dad found out that there was a club in town where they had live music three evenings a week, and he thought it might be useful to go because they might meet people who could put them in contact with musicians. They had been booked to video a wedding reception on the Saturday evening but as soon as it was over they went to the club to see a band called ‘Golden Cluster’.

“You got the right place, mate?” the young man who took their money said, looking at his dad’s Teddy Boy clothes. “It’s not Old Time Dancing Night, you know.”

“Listen, sonny,” his dad said, leaning over the counter and putting his face close to the young man’s, “if you don’t want to go ’ome to mummy wiv a couple of broken teeth just give us the tickets and shut your cakehole.”

The man backed away and slid the tickets across the counter. They went down the stairs and, as they pushed open the doors, a wave of hot, smoky air hit them. The room was dark except for two thin bright white beams flashing backwards and forwards over the heads of the packed audience.

Suddenly there was a crash of drums and the stage lights burst on. The singer had his back to the audience and was wearing a long black cloak but, as the deafening roar of music built up, he spun round and began shouting and screaming into the microphone. He flung the cloak off his shoulders to reveal that he was only wearing wellington boots and a pair of golden boxing shorts. He had smeared his body with white make-up that made him look like a ghost and there was a large black swastika painted on his chest.

Buddy barely had time to take it all in because his dad grabbed his arm and pulled him through the doors and up the stairs.

"'Ere you," his dad said throwing the tickets to the man at the entrance, "I'll 'ave me money back. I wanted music, not the zoo."

The man looked for a moment as if he were going to say something but he thought better of it and handed back the money without a word.

"I tell you what," his dad said on the way home, "if I see you on stage dressed up like that freak I'll knock your block off. I mean, moving around and dressing up flash is OK but that bloke needs 'is brain seeing to."

When they got home his mum asked what the group had been like and his dad started on about them all over again.

"Charming," she said, "and that's the world you want your son to go into – weirdos and drugs and stuff – when he could do something decent."

"Something boring, you mean," his dad snapped.

"There's nothing boring about a good education and a proper job. But you wouldn't know about that."

As Buddy listened to them arguing about what he should do, he could feel his temper rising. He was fed up with the way his mum always criticized music, but he was also fed up with the way his dad seemed to be taking charge of him all the time.

“Why don’t you both shut up,” he shouted suddenly, standing up and walking to the door. “You both talk about me as if I’m not here.”

They looked at him in surprise, but before they had a chance to say anything he went out of the door and slammed it behind him.

The more he thought about it over the next few days, the more it depressed him. He’d hoped that everything would be all right between them once his dad got out of prison, but recently they seemed to row every day. The big trouble was that he couldn’t decide which of them was right.

The whole idea of the future was confusing and frightening. When his mum talked about secure jobs and getting ahead, he always saw in his mind a picture of her boss. Even though he’d never met him, he hated Mr Mandell and the idea of ending up like him. But when he thought about taking risks like his dad said, he couldn’t help remembering those tramps on the industrial estate and wondering if he might end up like them, searching for squashed tomatoes in dustbins.

There had been times in the past when he couldn’t wait to get out of school and really start living, but now it seemed like a safe, easy place where no big decisions had to be taken. He was glad that he couldn’t leave until he was sixteen – that meant another term at least. In the meantime he could go on playing the guitar as a hobby because while there was no group to play with even his dad couldn’t pretend there was a future in music.

Two days later he had just woken up when he heard the front door open and the sound of his dad’s footsteps running up the stairs. He was usually tired after his night at the garage and Buddy jumped out of bed wondering if anything was wrong.

“’Ere, guess what!” his dad shouted, bursting through the door with a big smile on his face. “I’ve found a group.”

Buddy sat down on the edge of the bed in surprise and listened while his dad told him how he’d met an old friend called Dougie. They had talked about music and Dougie had mentioned a group he knew. His dad had immediately rung the leader and talked things over with him.

"It's all fixed," he said. "I've even got somewhere you can rehearse. This lot can never find a place, so I rang Des King and 'e's got this big shed up the breakers yard and 'e said we can use it any time. No 'ouses near, so we can make as much row as we like. It's me night off tomorrow so we're meeting 'em there at seven. Great, innit?"

Buddy was too stunned to do anything but smile weakly and nod.

The following evening his dad called a taxi to take them to the Industrial Estate because it was too far to lug the guitar and amplifier. All the way he grumbled about his job at the garage but Buddy was too nervous to listen. The big gate to the breakers yard was open and there were still people climbing among the piles of old and wrecked cars, searching for spare parts. His heart was pounding as he followed his dad along the muddy path towards the large new concrete shed that stood on one side of the enormous yard. There was a big caravan parked up against one wall, and in front of the doorway was a battered old transit van. Buddy thought it was one of the wrecks but as he got closer he could see, painted on the side in rough blue letters, the sign 'The Hi-Tone Four'.

They pulled the sliding door open and looked into the shed. At the far end were workbenches and piles of car spares – old engines, clutches and radiators. In front of this junk, 'The Hi-Tone Four' had already set up their equipment and were playing a waltz. Buddy took one look and started to back out of the door but his dad grabbed him.

"They don't just play this kind of music. They can do anything – Dougie told me."

"Yeah, but look at them," Buddy whispered. "I can't play with them."

He hadn't imagined what the group might be like because he had worried mainly about playing with other people, but he had assumed they would be quite young. Instead, they were all at least forty-five. The drummer was bald, the bass player and the guitarist had Teddy Boy haircuts like his dad except their greasy quiffs and sideburns were much greyer, and the sax player was so fat that his belly wobbled up and down as he played.

"Don't be daft," his dad said, holding on tight as Buddy tried to pull his arm free. "It'll be good experience. It's only a chance to muck around, that's all."

He dragged Buddy towards the group and they stopped playing.

"You Terry?" the sax player asked.

"That's right. And this is me kid, Buddy."

"Right," the sax player said, shaking their hands. "I'm Paul. Ernie on the drums. Phil on bass, and Barry on guitar." The men nodded at Buddy as they were introduced.

"Nice place you got here for us, Terry," Paul went on. "Good acoustics. It's a right pain trying to find somewhere to rehearse. Anyway, let's get on with it. Sing a bit, do you, son? OK, plug your amp in over there – the mike's all set up."

Buddy plugged in his amplifier and started to tune his guitar. His hands were trembling and his mouth had gone so dry that he felt as if he wouldn't be able to sing a note. Paul asked what he wanted to play and he thought quickly – something fast, something loud. If he could shout and jump around a bit he might relax.

"Do you know 'Rave On'?" he asked.

Paul laughed. "'Course we do. OK. 'Rave On', boys. Sixteen-bar sax intro then you sing, right? Ready. A-one, a-two, a-one, two, three, four."

There was a roll on the drums, a clash of cymbals, and Paul roared into the kind of old-style rock 'n' roll saxophone introduction that Buddy had heard on so many of his dad's records. He stood in front of the mike and bounced up and down to the rocking beat. His dad had got an old crate and was sitting on it about ten feet away. As the sax intro reached the end and Buddy leaned towards the mike, his dad flashed him a grin.

Buddy took a deep breath, closed his eyes, and launched into the song. He hit the beat perfectly and when he opened his eyes at the end of the first verse, he saw his dad on his feet, jumping up and down and punching the air in excitement. Buddy wanted to laugh but the pounding rhythm of the guitars and drums was pushing him into the chorus and the laugh came out on the word 'We-e-ell' as a perfect imitation of the sort of stuttery hiccough that Buddy Holly used to do in his singing. His dad let out a huge whoop of joy.

At the end of the chorus, Paul nudged Buddy away and started to blow a wild solo on the sax. When he finished and stepped aside, Buddy swung back to the mike and sang another verse and two choruses. He was lost in the music, feeling every note and every pulse of the rhythm. Barry played a quick guitar solo, then bent towards the mike and joined in to sing the last chorus. Instinctively, Buddy found himself singing a great harmony line. Paul honked and wailed a brief closing solo then, with a crash of drums and cymbals, the song was over.

The echo of the last notes faded away. There was a short silence as Buddy stood, almost dazed with the thrill of what had just happened. Then he heard his dad clapping and shouting "Yeah!" at the top of his voice.

There was a tap on his shoulder and Buddy turned round. Paul's face was glistening with sweat but his eyes were crinkled with a smile. "You're all right, son," he said. "A right little rocker. Now, let's see if you can sing something slow."

Buddy chose 'Raining in my Heart'. A-one, a-two, a-one, two, three, four . . .

From then on they alternated between belting rockers and slow songs. He even sang a couple of songs which Paul suggested. He'd never sung them before but Barry told him the chords and he was pleased to find that he picked them up very fast. They played for nearly an hour, then, when he tried for a high note at the end of a song, his voice went croaky.

"Better pack up now or you'll wreck your throat," Paul said, then walked over to talk to his dad.

It was true that his throat was a bit raw but nothing he had ever done before had given him such a kick, and he felt as if he could go on playing for ever. He turned to Barry and asked him to show him some different chords that he'd noticed him doing. He was still trying them out when his dad put his arm round his shoulder.

"Come on, mate – we're off home. Leave your gear 'ere. Des said he'd lock up. Save you 'aving to cart it back tomorrow."

"Tomorrow?"

"That's right," Paul said. "Got a bit of rehearsing to do before Saturday week. You go home and gargle, son. Got to keep them vocal chords of yours in shape."

The full moon was high and its glow lit up the deserted warehouses as they walked through the empty streets of the industrial estate. Buddy was so wound up with excitement and happiness that he didn't want to speak. His whole body felt electric and everything seemed magical – the cool night air on his face, the smooth hump of the bridge over the river, the moonlight on the water, even the sharp click of their footsteps echoing back from the dark buildings. They were nearly home before he asked, "Dad, what's all this about Saturday week?"

"Oh that – well, one of the geezers who's hired us to video his daughter's wedding asked me to find a band for the party after. And I've asked Paul."

"But why have I got to rehearse?"

"'Cos you're gonna do an 'alf hour spot wiv 'em, that's why."

Buddy stopped, but before he could say anything his dad went on. "Now don't moan – you've got to do it. I promised the geezer I'd get a band who could play stuff for everyone. Well, Paul can 'andle the waltzes and cha-chas an' all that, but 'e ain't got no one to sing stuff for the kids to dance to."

Buddy didn't know whether to laugh or be angry. "You told me this evening it was just mucking about. You set the whole thing up, didn't you?"

His dad winked cheekily. "Sneaky beggar, ain't I? Anyway, just think – in eight days' time you're gonna do your first gig. It's gonna be a big day. More than big – it's gonna be flippin' historical!"

15

Buddy rehearsed with 'The Hi-Tone Four' every evening for a week. He and Paul selected twelve songs for the set and they went over them again and again, trying out various tempos and deciding who would play the solos. He enjoyed the rehearsals and he could hear that his singing and playing were improving but, somehow, it was never as exciting as the first evening, and he never felt as lost in the music as he had done then.

"That was because it was the first time and you were all keyed up," Paul said. "You just wait until you get in front of an audience . . . You'll feel completely different."

In fact, sitting on the side of the stage on the Saturday evening, Buddy did feel different – he felt awful. All day long he had been nervous, but when they arrived at the church hall and set up the equipment his stomach suddenly heaved and he had to rush to the nearest lavatory to be sick. Now, waiting for the moment when Paul would call him on stage, all he wanted to do was run home and never think of singing again. His heart was pounding so fast that it seemed to shake his whole body and each time he took a breath his stomach muscles trembled. His hands were damp with sweat and he was sure that he would never be able to control his fingers to make the chords.

The band was playing a dance number called 'Perfidia' and he knew that it was the last song before he went on. He stood up and peered through the side of the curtain.

There were about a hundred people in the hall – a few of them dancing, but most of them still crowding round the buffet table and the bar, laughing and talking and hardly paying any attention to the music. Perhaps, he found himself hoping, nobody would even notice him while he sang.

The band came to the end of 'Perfidia' and Buddy watched as Paul stepped up to the microphone.

"Thank you, ladies and gentlemen, boys and girls. Now, I hope you're all in the mood for a bit of moving and grooving because we're going to change the tempo. I'd like to introduce a young man who's making his first appearance on stage tonight. I know you're going to love him – so let's have a warm welcome, please, for Buddy Clark."

Buddy slipped the guitar strap over his head and walked on stage. He was aware of one person clapping very loudly and whistling, and out of the corner of his eye he saw it was his dad, standing in front of the stage. Nobody else joined in the applause and Buddy felt his knees almost give way under him.

Why had he ever allowed himself to be roped into this? It was going to be a disaster, he knew it. He plugged his guitar into the amp and walked to the microphone. Luckily, with the spotlight shining in his eyes, he couldn't actually see out into the hall. He would pretend there was nobody there, sing his songs as quickly as possible, get out of there and never come back.

He turned and nodded to the group to show that he was ready. Ernie tapped out the beat on the cymbal, Phil's bass began to boom and then, just as they had rehearsed it, Paul blew just one loud honk on the sax. In the half-beat of silence that followed, Buddy swung round to the mike and, with only the cymbal beating time, he belted into the first four lines of 'Rip It Up'.

It felt lonely, just him and the cymbal, but as he reached the first chorus the band blasted in to join him and he was lifted on the wave of sound. The rimshot crashes of the drums, the throbbing of the bass and the stabbing chords of Barry's guitar drove the song forward and he went with it – all nerves gone, as he lost himself in the joyous beat.

All evening he'd been worrying about forgetting the words but they poured out of him easily and, just like that first time, he found himself charged with energy. He knew that he had started to jump around to the music but he didn't care; even if he tried, he couldn't stop. When it came to Paul's sax solo, Buddy let out an unrehearsed whoop into the microphone then jumped aside and began dancing across the stage towards Barry. They pointed their guitars at each other and Barry smiled in delight and started to jump up and down while the sax solo roared out.

As he skipped and danced his way back to the mike, Buddy glanced down into the hall and saw that the floor was packed with moving bodies. Great! All he wanted to do was sing and make people dance, so he threw himself into the second part of the song.

He hit the final note, the sax screamed, the drums rattled into one last crash, and it was all over. He stood panting in front of the microphone and heard the applause roll towards him. This time it wasn't just his dad – it was everyone. But Buddy wasn't interested. All he wanted to do was sing, and before the clapping had faded away, he had stamped out the beat with his foot and led the band into the second song.

When he came to the last song of the set, Buddy noticed that there were three girls standing just in front of the stage. They were clapping their hands to the beat and staring straight up into his face, and whenever he looked down at them they smiled. A thrill shot through him and, as he struck the last chord, he whirled round and leaped into the air with his guitar held up high over his head. He glanced down and saw that the girls were clutching each other and screaming.

Hours later, when he sat at home and watched the video his dad had made of the set, his mum laughed out loud when she saw the bit where he leaped into the air.

"Cor, you little sexpot," she said. "Look what you did to those girls – they're going bananas."

"The whole flipping audience went bananas," his dad said, switching off the video and putting his arm round Buddy. "You should've heard 'em. They loved 'im."

"Well?" Buddy asked, looking at his mum.

"Well, I think it looks dead stupid, a kid of your age playing with a group of old blokes like that, but . . ." she smiled and patted him on the cheek, "I have to admit, it wasn't bad."

"Not bad? Don't talk rubbish, Carol, he was knockout."

"All right, he was good. But if you go on like that, his head'll get so big it'll drop off. And I do think it looks weird, him playing with those old codger friends of yours."

"They're not my friends – they're Dougie's. And anyway, that's just a start. We'll find a proper group for 'im later. The point is, 'e was terrific. I tell you, 'e's gonna be a star. Just mark my words, everything's gonna change from now on."

Everything did change. It changed fast, and it changed for the worse. Buddy could hardly believe how quickly he could go from feeling so good and full of hope, to feeling so bad and hopeless. It happened in less than a week.

The week began well enough. He went for a rehearsal with 'The Hi-Tone Four' on the Monday, and Paul and the others all went on about what a great gig it had been and how well he had done. They practised for a couple of hours, but they were in such a good mood that they mostly mucked around, trying out songs they hadn't played before and generally having a laugh.

Buddy felt fine when he got home but as he opened the front door he walked straight into a row.

His dad had chucked up the job at the garage. His mum was upset that he hadn't given a week's notice as he was supposed to, but what she was really angry about was that he'd got a new job, working for Des King.

"Look, 'ow many times do I 'ave to tell you?" his dad yelled. "There's nuffin' bent about it. I'm driving a truck, delivering and fetching car parts, that's all. Regular hours – eight-thirty to five, nearly twice as much money as the garage pays. I tell you, I'd be a mug not to take it. It's dead straight, I swear."

"Des King doesn't do anything straight. I know him, Terry, and I know you. Once he gets his claws on you again, you're finished. When he tells you 'jump', you're too weak to do anything but jump."

Buddy went to bed and tried to cut out the noise of the row by pulling the pillow over his ears.

The next day there was another row when his mum got home from work and saw the large pick-up truck, marked 'King's Breakers', parked outside the house. His dad was having a bath but she went straight upstairs, burst into the bathroom, and started shouting that she didn't want the truck left there where all the neighbours could see he was working for a thief. When Buddy heard his dad shouting back that he wasn't going to walk miles to work just because she'd become a snob, he decided to go out.

He went into town just to get out of the house, but when he got there he didn't know what to do. At one time he could have gone round to see the Rybeero twins, but now there was nowhere to go. In the end he went to the cinema and sat through a stupid film about people trying to rob a bank. The last shot of the film was of prison gates closing as the robbers were driven inside. It seemed like a terrible omen.

When he got home, his mum was already in bed and his dad was slumped on the sofa watching telly. Buddy said hello but his dad just grunted and went on staring at the screen, so he had a drink of milk and went to bed.

The next three days were tense and nobody said very much, but at least there were no scenes. Buddy sensed in advance, though, that there could be trouble on the Friday. Weeks before, his mum had been invited to a dinner party at Joyce's flat and when his dad had reluctantly agreed to go she had put a big ring round the date on the calendar.

The trouble began as they were getting ready. His dad stayed out in his workshed until the last minute and then had to rush to wash and change in time. His mum was obviously annoyed but she didn't say anything until she saw that he was putting on jeans.

"You can't go like that, Terry."

"Why the 'ell not?"

"Oh grow up – this is a dinner party, not a tramps' picnic."

"I don't care if it's Christmas lunch wiv the Queen. I'm going in me jeans, or I ain't going."

They argued about this for a few minutes but when his mum found out that he hadn't ordered a taxi as he had promised and that they were going in the truck, she really hit the roof. It was too late to call a taxi, though, and they left the house still arguing. Buddy watched them drive off in the truck, then sat down to watch TV. There was nothing good on so he decided to watch the video of the wedding gig. Usually he enjoyed it but tonight he couldn't help noticing how silly he looked prancing up and down with a group of old men playing behind him.

He switched the TV off and went upstairs to play his old guitar but his heart wasn't in it. He put the guitar down and tried to read but he couldn't concentrate on the book either. The only thing he could think about was what might be happening at Joyce's flat. His mum and dad were both in such foul moods that he wouldn't put it past them to spend the whole evening rowing. It was all his dad's fault really. It wouldn't have hurt him to dress up a bit smart for something that his mum had been looking forward to so much. She'd looked very pretty in a new blue dress with matching shoes and handbag and he'd just looked sloppy in jeans and a crumpled sweat-shirt. On the other hand, he couldn't understand all the fuss about the truck – it did seem silly to waste money on a taxi when they had their own form of transport.

At just gone ten, there was a scream of tyres outside, followed by the slamming of doors. Out of his bedroom window he saw his mum running up the path while his dad stood in the street shouting something at her. For the next hour the shouting came from both of them, all over the house. Buddy could hear them wherever they were – in the kitchen, on the stairs, or in their bedroom. From what he could gather, his dad had behaved badly and said some nasty things to Joyce, but that wasn't what they were really rowing about. All their disagreements came pouring out. His mum went on about the job, the truck, the music, the clothes he wore; while his dad complained that she had changed and now she wanted to change him.

Suddenly there was a crash of glass followed by silence and, in panic, Buddy ran downstairs to the kitchen. His dad was sitting at the table and his mum was on her knees next to the fridge, picking up bits of a milk bottle.

"What happened?" he asked.

"Nothing, love – I just dropped it," his mum said.

"Good job it weren't me," his dad snarled, "or I'd never 'ave 'eard the last of it."

His mum swung round quickly to say something and caught her hand on a bit of jagged glass. She cried out in pain and a drop of blood splattered into the pool of spilt milk. Buddy started towards her, but his dad got there first. He bent down to help her but she pushed him away.

"Just leave me alone," she yelled, standing up and tearing off some kitchen paper to dab the cut.

His dad stood helpless for a moment then, as the paper became blood-soaked, he tore some more off and held it out towards her.

"Come on, Carol, let me do it."

"Look, can't you get it through your thick head – I don't need you," she shouted, her eyes blazing.

His dad stepped back with a hurt look on his face, and the paper dropped from his hands.

"Do you mean that?" he asked quietly. "Carol, do you mean that?"

His mum turned to the sink and began running water over the cut.

“Well, if you don’t need me, I’d better go then, ’adn’t I?” his dad mumbled.

His mum shrugged and said, “Suit yourself.”

Buddy watched numbly as his dad went to the table, picked up his coat, and walked past him to the front door. He opened it, stepped outside, and closed it behind him. A few moments later the truck roared away down the street.

His mum stayed at the sink, with her hand held under the running water.

“Mum,” he said, when she still didn’t move.

“Go to bed, Buddy. Please. I don’t want to talk.”

He stayed awake for ages. He heard her come upstairs and go to bed, but hours later when he finally drifted off to sleep the truck still hadn’t come back.

The following morning, he jumped out of bed and ran to the window. The truck wasn’t there. He had just finished dressing when there was a noise at the front door and he rushed downstairs, hoping it was his dad. There was a letter lying on the doormat. He picked it up. It was addressed to him. While he tore it open he glanced into the kitchen – the broken bottle and milk were still on the floor.

He pulled the letter out of the envelope and read it. It was his exam results. He had passed them all. He threw the letter on to the bottom step of the staircase, slipped his coat on, and opened the front door. The exam results didn’t matter. Nothing mattered, except finding out where his dad was.

16

There was only one place he could think of looking – the breakers yard. He walked quickly, unable to stop himself from worrying about crashes. His dad had been in such a state, anything could have happened. When he reached the yard, though,there was the pick-up truck parked in front of the shed.

The truck was empty and he was just going to look in the shed when he noticed that the door of the caravan was open. He climbed the two steps and saw his dad lying on a bunk, with his arms across his face. He sat up as the caravan shook under Buddy's weight.

"Oh, it's you," his dad said and lay down again. "Did she send you?"

Buddy shook his head and sat down on the other bunk. There was a sink and a small gas cooker near the door, the two bunks, a table and a couple of benches at the far end.

"Is this where you slept?"

"No, the gates were locked – I 'ad to kip in the truck. Des says I can stay 'ere, though. There's a toilet and a sink at the back of the shed – 'ot water, too. Everyfing you need. Cooker, electricity – the lot."

He rolled over and turned his face to the wall. Buddy sat for a long time waiting for him to say something.

"Aren't you coming back, then?" he asked at last.

"You 'eard what she said – she don't need me."

He wanted to say that it wasn't true, that she'd only said it in anger, that everything would be all right, but he couldn't. Things had become so bad recently that, much as he hated the idea, perhaps it would be better if his mum and dad didn't see each other for a while.

There was a loud clanking noise outside and, through the window, he watched a large crane reach down and pick up a car in its claws. The side windows shattered and the roof buckled as the claws closed on the car and it was lifted up and swung round to be dumped on a pile of wrecks.

He sat watching the activity in the yard for nearly a quarter of an hour, hoping that his dad would say something, but he just lay in the same position facing the wall.

"Dad," he said quietly, wondering if he'd fallen asleep. "Are you going to stay here?"

His dad nodded.

"Shall I tell Mum where you are?"

His dad shrugged. There was no point in asking anything else so he got up and walked to the door.

"Buddy," his dad said, still not moving. "Come and see me sometimes, will you?"

"'Course I will."

"We've still got the music, ain't we?" his dad said, turning over and smiling sadly at him.

"'Course we have."

His dad nodded, then rolled back to face the wall.

When he got back home his mum was sitting at the kitchen table drinking a cup of coffee. She picked up a spoon and started stirring the coffee while he told her about his dad. Round and round went the spoon, clinking against the side of the cup and sending little waves of coffee spilling over the rim into the saucer. When he finished speaking she went on stirring and he was just about to tell her to stop when she lifted the spoon and, with trembling fingers, put it to her lips. She sipped the coffee, laid the spoon in the flooded saucer, and picked up a piece of paper.

It was the exam results. She held it up to him and, raising her eyes, she tried to smile.

"You did brilliant," she said, then burst out crying. She slumped forward on to the table and her shoulders heaved with sobs. He moved across and gently rubbed the top of her arm but she shrank away from his touch.

"Don't," she moaned. "Don't be nice to me. I don't deserve it. Oh, Buddy, you worked so hard and now . . ."

Her sobs grew more violent and he stood watching helplessly as his own eyes filled with tears. He wanted to hold her but, scared it might make her worse, he bent down and picked up the pieces of broken bottle that still lay on the floor, then tore off some kitchen paper and mopped up the milk.

"Give me some tissues," she said, sitting up and wiping her face roughly on the sleeves of her dressing-gown. She blew her nose hard on the tissue, then crushed the paper in her right hand and held it as if it might help her to stop the tears.

"I tried," she said, her voice flat and calm, although the tears still ran freely down her cheeks. "I really tried. But it's no good. He says I've changed and it's true. I have. But I can't help it and I can't go back. He's the same, and I'm not. That's all."

She sniffed and dabbed her face. She blinked the last tear from her eye and stared ahead. Buddy watched the tear trickle down past her nose then, as it ran past her mouth, she sucked her bottom lip between her teeth and sighed. He saw the tear drop and melt into the bobbly blue material of the sleeve of her dressing-gown.

"Do you think I'm wrong?" she said, taking his hand.

He shrugged.

"You do! You think I'm wrong. You're on his side."

"I'm not. Why does it have to be sides?"

She shook her head and let go of his hand . "I don't know – it just seems like that. He wants you to do the music and everything and I . . . I know his ideas sound more exciting, but I love you, too, Buddy, and I want the best for you."

"I know you do."
"He's always been like that – exciting and full of ideas. I remember when I first met him . . ." Her voice trailed off and a faint smile flickered across her lips, but then she shook her head and her mouth became unhappy again.
"Look at him, though – where did it ever get him?"
Buddy couldn't stay to hear anymore. If she went on like this, he would cry.
"Where are you going?" she asked as he went to the door.
"To play my guitar."
"Buddy, don't be upset."
"I'm not."
He played the guitar loud and fast, pressing his fingertips hard on to the strings so they hurt. He wouldn't cry. He wouldn't.
When his mum came in later, he forced himself to seem happy.
"I'm going out, love. I want to go round and see . . .", she paused and for a moment Buddy hoped she was going to say dad, ". . . to see Joyce and have a talk. You don't mind, do you?"
He smiled and shook his head.
He kept on playing until he heard her leave the house, then he put the guitar down and lay on his bed listening to the silence. His brain was buzzing wildly with what had happened and he felt as if he wanted to scream. Then, three words came into his mind – torn in half. He sat up, picked up his guitar and began to play some chords, singing those words to himself like a chant. Then he added another phrase – try to laugh. He chanted the two lines and, gradually, other words came.
Finally he grabbed a pen and wrote down what he'd been singing.

> You're telling me your stories,
> You're handing me a line.
> You're giving me your point of view

But you never think of mine.
You tell me that you love me,
You say I ought to laugh.
Why is it that you just can't see
That I am torn in half.
I try to laugh
But I'm torn in half.

It helped to sing it and he sang it over and over, adding more and more lines until he had written a song. His song.

It was a change to get back to school and worry about small things like what subjects he was going to do at 'A' level. He wanted to do maths and physics and English, but the teacher in charge of the sixth form tried to get him to drop the English and do another science subject, because it would be easier to time-table. In the end, though, they managed to fit it in – although he would have to miss a couple of physics lessons which the teacher said he'd have to catch up on his own.

He liked some of the things about being in the sixth form. There was a special common room, you didn't have to wear uniform, and the whole atmosphere was freer – but because he'd missed out the fifth year he was a year younger than the other pupils and he felt out of place. It was all rather like when he'd been promoted to the express stream in the second year. Then, he had found himself in a class with people who came from the posh end of town – they talked differently from him, dressed differently and seemed to live completely different lives. As far as he could see, the people in the sixth and seventh years all came from the express stream and they made him feel unwelcome all over again. On top of that, nobody else was doing the same combination of subjects so it was hard to get to know anyone.

Then, slowly, he began to talk to some of the other people and he found a few who were interested in music. He always sat with them in the common room and he even got invited to a party, but it was on a Saturday when he was helping his dad video a wedding reception, so he couldn't go.

Now that summer was over, there were fewer weddings and his dad only managed to get 'The Hi-Tone Four' a couple of gigs at receptions during the whole Autumn term. The gigs and the occasional rehearsals were still the highspots of his life but Buddy began to feel that he wasn't really getting anywhere with the group because they were content to go on playing the same things all the time. More and more, he was enjoying writing his own songs – though his dad never seemed to think much of them when he played them to him.

He visited the caravan at least three or four evenings a week – especially when his mum was working late, as she did quite often – and he liked sitting there playing the guitar or watching the small portable TV his dad had bought. In a strange way the caravan, though it usually looked a tip because his dad never tidied up, seemed more cosy and friendly than the house. Sometimes his dad would open up a couple of cans of beer and they would sprawl on the bunks and watch TV or listen to music and chat about things. They never talked about his mum, but his dad seemed quite happy living on his own and he said that if he ever got lonely he went down to the pub and met his friends.

His mum, on the other hand, always asked how his dad was. She wanted to know things like whether he was eating OK and how he did his washing and if the caravan was warm enough. Once when she was talking about his dad, Buddy asked her if she would like him to come home but she just shrugged her shoulders and changed the subject. Gradually, as the months passed, he got used to them living apart and he stopped hoping that something would change and they would get together again.

The only really bad times were on special days. It was horrible, for example, that they weren't all together for his sixteenth birthday. He spent the early part of the evening with his dad who insisted on taking him down to the pub to celebrate. Some of his dad's mates were there and they sang 'Happy Birthday' while his dad handed over a present – a beautiful embossed leather guitar strap. He wanted him to stay all evening but Buddy explained that he had to get home because his mum was cooking a special meal.

"Oh well," his dad said sarcastically, "you'd better not keep madam waiting or she'll do 'er nut."

His mum made him steak and chips, and at the end of the meal she gave him her present. It was a book – *The Complete Plays of Shakespeare.* She had bought a bottle of wine and he drank a couple of glasses. On top of the two pints of beer he'd had earlier it made him feel quite drunk. At first he was light-headed and happy then, while they were washing up, he suddenly felt sad and he blurted out what he'd been thinking all day.

"I haven't had a birthday with you and dad since I was thirteen."

She sighed and put her arms round him and kissed him on the cheek. "Buddy, don't make me feel bad," she said softly.

At Christmas his dad decided to spend the time with some friends so, once again, Buddy and his mum went round to Joyce's flat. They had a great lunch but in the middle of the afternoon Joyce got a migraine and had to go and lie down. Buddy and his mum sat for a while talking quietly so as not to disturb her, but when it became obvious that she wasn't getting better and would rather sleep, they went home. The house was cold, there were no decorations and it wasn't like Christmas at all. They ate sandwiches, watched TV, and went to bed early.

Because he'd spent Christmas with his mum, he spent New Year's Eve with his dad. They went out to the cinema and then dropped into the pub and had a drink with his dad's friends. When they got back to the caravan, his dad opened a couple of cans of beer and switched on the telly. Midnight was chiming on Big Ben and people were dancing in Trafalgar Square and his dad grabbed hold of him and made him join in the singing. Buddy felt awkward and embarrassed as he swayed back and forth with his dad's arm round his shoulder, and he couldn't help thinking how silly they must look, singing 'Auld Lang Syne' in a caravan surrounded by piles of wrecked cars.

When the song ended, his dad switched off the telly. His face looked suddenly old and sad as he turned to Buddy and raised his can of beer. "Let's drink to absent friends," he said. "To your mum and to . . . anyway, to absent friends. Come on, drink up."

Buddy had arranged to spend the night, and when they finally went to bed he lay in the dark in his sleeping-bag and listened as his dad kept moving restlessly on the other bunk.

"Buddy," his dad said at last. "Do you mind being an only kid?"

"What do you mean?"

"You know – would you 'ave liked to 'ave bruvvers and sisters?"

"Never thought about it."

There was a long silence then his dad's voice came again in the darkness, so quietly that Buddy had to strain to hear it.

"Don't never say nuffin' to your mum. She don't like to talk about it – that's why we never told you. You 'ad a bruvver."

A tingle ran across Buddy's forehead and into his scalp as he listened to his dad's voice whispering so sadly in the night.

"'E was born on New Year's Day. Not somefing you can forget, that. Tiny little thing 'e was. I only saw 'im once. 'Ad somefing the matter wiv 'is 'eart, poor little kid. Only lived five hours. 'E would've been fourteen today." His dad sniffed and sighed. "Ain't fair, is it? To never get a chance like that. That's why I think sometimes, 'Terry, you're alive – you got the chance to do somefing; not like that little kid who only 'ad five hours'."

Buddy looked over at his dad's face silhouetted against the moonlight pouring in through the caravan window. His dad raised his hand and wiped his eyes, then turned and looked at him.

"Buddy, we got a lot of living to do, you and me," he said, his voice stronger again now. "Let's make it a good year, eh?"

Buddy leaned his arm across the gap between them and his dad took hold of his hand and squeezed.

"'Night, son."

"'Night, Dad."

17

Buddy noticed the twins on the first morning back at school – not that they looked a bit like twins. He just saw two new faces in the common room and, attracted by the idea of meeting people who hadn't grown up in the school, he walked across and introduced himself.

"Hi," said the taller of the two, in a strong northern accent. "I'm Mike. This is my brother, Jason."

Jason was thin, with a long narrow face framed by black hair almost down to his shoulders. He had on two big silver earrings and was wearing a maroon bomber jacket, a floppy T-shirt and jeans, whereas Mike was dressed much more formally in grey trousers, a white shirt and dark blue jumper.

"You don't look like brothers," Buddy said, knowing it sounded stupid.

"We're very unidentical twins," Jason said in a bored voice, then turned away to look out of the window. His fingers tapped out a rhythm on the tiles of the windowsill.

Buddy felt as if Jason had taken one look and dismissed him, but Mike was much friendlier and seemed almost anxious to talk about himself and his brother. They were seventeen and this was their fourth school in five years because their father's job took him all over the country. Their last school had been in Plymouth and they were both doing History, Geography and Commerce at 'A' level.

The bell rang for the first lesson and Buddy went off, intending to talk to them at break. The fact that they were twins appealed to him. His only good friends at school had been the Rybeero twins – perhaps it was an omen. In fact, he wasn't able to talk to them again until the end of the week. They were never in the Common Room when he was, and he only glimpsed them a couple of times in the corridor.

Then, on Friday afternoon, he stayed late in the library searching for books for an English essay he had to do. He was on his way out of the school when he heard music coming from the gym. He pushed open the door and saw the twins.

Jason was leaning against the wallbars plucking a bass, while Mike was sitting on a vaulting horse, playing an electric guitar. It was a slow blues tune and Mike was chugging away at a simple blues riff but, after a moment, he jumped down from the horse and began a wailing solo while Jason's bass broke into a more forceful rocking beat. They were good and Buddy watched in admiration, wishing he had his guitar with him and could join in.

The twins were so caught up in the music that they didn't notice him until they had finished. When they saw him, Jason turned away and started playing bass runs to himself but Mike smiled and waved him over.

"It was great," Buddy said. "Made me want to join in."

"Hey, you don't play keyboards do you?" Mike asked.

"No. Rhythm guitar."

"Pity. We're looking for someone on keyboards and drums. We had a group down in Plymouth and this guy played great synthesizer. We want to start something up here, but we'll never find anyone as good."

"I sing a bit, too," Buddy said.

"So do I," Jason said, giving him a really hostile glare.

"Yeah, well – anyway . . ." Buddy said, beginning to move towards the door.

"Hey," Mike called. "Don't mind Jas. He's a moody pig. Bring your gear in on Monday – we can have a muck-around."

"Sure," Buddy said, then looked at Jason. "OK?"

Jason slapped a few notes on his bass then nodded. "Yeah, why not?"

They met up in the gym at four on the Monday and sat around talking for a while, all slightly nervous at the idea of starting. Buddy mentioned the gigs with 'The Hi-Tone Four' but he was careful not to say anything about how old the rest of the group were. Mike told him about the group they'd had in Plymouth. They'd done some gigs in pubs and youth clubs, playing all kinds of music from modern pop to Soul and even a bit of Heavy Metal. The group had just started to make a reputation when the twins had had to leave.

"Now we've got to start all over again," Jason said.

"Would you like to go into music full-time?" Buddy asked.

"Too damn right. Wouldn't you?"

Buddy nodded and Jason burst into a big smile – the first time Buddy had seen him look anything but miserable.

"Oh, wouldn't it be great?" Jason went on. "Records, gigs – I just don't want anything else. Come on. Let's stop rabbiting and play something."

The session started quietly. Buddy was content to let the twins choose the songs and, since they were all new to him, he just strummed along trying to follow the chord changes and adapt to the different style. He felt nervous but he didn't allow himself to be put off, even when Jason glanced in annoyance as he fumbled over a chord sequence and lost the rhythm.

Then Jason decided to sing. The first song he chose was one that Buddy knew so, at last, he felt confident and could let the rhythm take him over. He was aware that his guitar playing started to swing to a more positive beat and at the end Jason gave him an approving nod. It was the sign that Buddy had been looking for and he asked if they could play the song again and let him sing it. They agreed and Buddy took his place in front of the microphone. Jason had sung quite well but Buddy knew he could do better.

"Let's try it a bit faster," he said, and tapped them into a quicker tempo. He let go with one of the opening yells he'd learned to do with 'The Hi-Tone Four' then launched into a wild, rocking version of the song. There were no drums to pound out the beat but that made him sing even more strongly and after a couple of bars the twins responded. Jason's bass began to rock and Mike started to play some runs on the guitar.

By the time they were halfway through, the music lifted off and Buddy couldn't stand still. He danced and roared his way to the end of a verse and when he glanced round he saw Jason bouncing up and down with his eyes closed, completely lost in the beat. Mike picked up a metal finger-piece and swung into a fiery slide guitar solo that echoed the way Buddy had been singing. The solo soared to an end and Buddy took over for another verse and chorus, inspired by the push that the guitar sound had given him.

When the song finished, there was that second or so of silence that always seemed to happen when a song went well – as if it took a moment to come back to earth. Then Jason began to laugh.

"Whooo! Hey, that took off. Boy, you can really sing. Can't he, Mike?"

He was tugging at his brother's sleeve like an excited little boy. Mike's eyes were shining and he was grinning broadly.

"That was fantastic," he said, shaking his head as if he couldn't take it in. "Wow, you really rock!"

They all stood there for a moment, smiling foolishly at each other with pleasure at what had taken place, then Jason plucked a note on his bass and shouted, "Well, come on, then – let's play some more."

From then on, they met for about an hour every day after school. The twins had never played the old rock 'n' roll stuff but gradually Buddy introduced all the songs he knew and they grew to like them a lot. He was particularly pleased when he decided to try out his own song, 'Torn In Half', and they thought it was great. Mike suggested that they should write more of their own songs and nearly every day one of them brought in something to try out. Some of them didn't work, but a few were worth keeping and they spent time changing the words or trying different melodies. At the same time, the twins taught Buddy all the songs they knew so that they soon had a large repertoire to draw on.

He found that his own guitar playing improved rapidly with the constant practice, but what gave him most pleasure was the singing. Most of the songs he'd learned from the twins were in a different style from those he sang with 'The Hi-Tone Four' and day by day he could sense his voice becoming stronger and more confident. On top of that, Jason's voice blended well with his, and they enjoyed singing in harmony on choruses of the fast numbers. They even did close harmony duets on slow love songs.

The music brought them together quickly and, as he got to know them better, Buddy noticed that the twins had totally opposite temperaments. Mike was always easy-going and friendly during the day but he often became tense and argumentative about the music. He had strong ideas about how things should sound and he often bossed Buddy and his brother until he got his way. Jason, on the other hand, was incredibly moody at school, sometimes hardly speaking to people, yet he seemed to come alive as soon as they got together to play. He danced to the music, his long hair swinging round his face, his eyes closed, and his lips curled into a smile of pleasure.

In between songs, he was the one who cracked jokes and poured out all his dreams of making it in the music business, so it wasn't surprising that he was the one who finally said, "Listen, we've just got to get out on the road and play gigs. There's a DJ on the local radio who makes announcements about groups looking for players. I'm going to send him a letter saying that we need a drummer and a keyboards player, and I'm going to put an ad in the music shop, too."

Sure enough, the following week Jason came into school with his cassette player and they listened to the recording of the DJ announcing that a young group wanted people to play drums and keyboards. It gave them all such a thrill that they played the tape over and over, laughing and pushing each other in excitement each time they heard it. They were even more excited when, within a few days, they got fifteen phone calls in reply to their ads.

It was a strange experience, knocking on strangers' doors and going inside to listen to them, and they often found it hard not to laugh at it all. One of the drummers, for example, was a boy of thirteen who had set up his kit in his bedroom and the entire time he was playing for them, his father kept calling up the stairs telling him to stop the noise. In the end, the boy kicked his bass drum over and started to argue with his father on the stairs while the three of them tried to get past to the front door. One of the keyboards players turned out to be a very old man who had set up an electric organ in his garage. He sat playing the organ, wearing a furry Russian hat, and singing strange songs in a deep voice, while Buddy and the twins struggled to keep straight faces.

Finally they found a drummer. Glenn was eighteen, with very short, spiky hair and tattoos covering his arms. He had left school and was working as a milkman. Almost every other word he used was a swear word. He seemed much older than his age and obviously wanted to impress them as being hard. On the other hand, although he had never played with a group, his drumming was terrific and he could vary from a gentle rhythm backing to wild, crashing sounds that rocked like mad.

"He's a bit loony, of course," Mike said after they'd seen him, "but I reckon you need a wild man on drums. I'm for trying him."

Buddy and Jason agreed, so Glenn became part of the group that was now known as 'The Reflections'. Mike had chosen the name and although Buddy didn't like it much he couldn't come up with anything better. The fact that Glenn finished his milk-round early meant that he could join them every day after school for their rehearsals in the gym, but first they had to ask permission from the head-mistress. She agreed but said that they were responsible for making sure Glenn behaved himself properly on the school premises. Buddy had his doubts whether anyone could force Glenn to do anything, but as it turned out he was rather awed by being back in a school and was always on his best behaviour.

Once he got behind his drums he became, as Mike had said, a wild man. His arms flailed and he rocked up and down on his stool, pounding away at the kit, so that he was always covered in sweat by the end of the first song. He had enormous energy, though, and was always ready to go on when the rest of them were exhausted. He also learned fast. At the end of the trial week they voted unanimously to keep him and when they told him, he was so pleased that he dropped the hard-nut act and blushed.

"Really?" he asked in surprise. When they repeated the offer he grabbed his drumsticks and beat a furious tattoo on the drums. As he finished, he threw the sticks high in the air, caught them, then sat back on his stool and grinned widely showing his missing front tooth.

But the group still hadn't found a keyboard player. They'd seen two whom Buddy had thought weren't bad, but the twins said they were useless compared with their friend Dave from Plymouth.

"There's no point in getting someone second-rate," Mike said.

"I agree," said Jason. "Better to start off with four people who are good and find someone else later. Anyway, I think the most important thing is getting a manager

– somebody to push us. And we won't get one until we've done some gigs. I don't know about you lot, but I want to get in front of an audience."

"Me, too," Buddy said.

Glenn did a fast roll on the drums, crashed a cymbal, and shouted, "Look out, world – here we come!"

18

The first gig that 'The Reflections' played was at a youth club near the docks. They all felt rather flat when they saw the bare, ugly hall. Setting up their equipment on the old wooden stage they found there was hardly enough room to move. They checked the sound level then closed the moth-eaten curtains and went into the small back-room to wait for the audience to arrive.

There were only a couple of chairs in the room and Jason and Glenn nearly had a row about who should sit on them. Mike solved the problem by pushing the chairs outside so they all had to sit on the dusty floor. Buddy pointed to a half-eaten sandwich in the corner but nobody thought it was funny and, as his nerves began to jangle, the sight of the sandwich made him feel sick. Eventually he got up and, his stomach heaving, he scraped the bits of bread and squashed egg off the floor and threw it out of the window.

Just at that moment there was a clank of opening doors and they heard the audience coming into the hall. A shiver ran down Buddy's back and he rushed out to the lavatory to be sick. When he returned, the other three looked as pale as he felt. Mike was pacing up and down on one side of the room, running his tongue nervously over his lips and brushing his hair back with his hands. Jason was pacing up and down on the other side of the room with his hands on his head, breathing deeply; while Glenn, almost green with fright, was sitting beating out a crazy rhythm on his knees.

"We'll be ready for you in five minutes," the Youth Leader said, popping his head round the door. "It's great – we're packed out already."

Buddy's mouth went completely dry and he knew he had to drink or his throat would seize up. He went out to the lavatory again, ran the tap in the wash-basin and scooped some water into his mouth. It was warm and his stomach heaved. He ran into the cubicle and leaned over the lavatory to be sick but nothing came. He was standing there, trembling, with a cold sweat on his face, when the door opened and Mike yelled, "Come on, we're on!"

He staggered to the door and saw the others climbing the wobbly stairs on to the stage. The curtains were already open and there were a few catcalls and jeers as the crowd saw them. Glenn tried to squeeze past his drum kit to get to his stool. He stumbled and sent one of his cymbals crashing to the ground. There was a loud laugh and some whistles but Glenn calmly picked up the cymbal, grinned at the audience, sat on his stool and raised his drumsticks high over his head. The audience went quiet, waiting to see what he would do. He brought the sticks crashing down on to the snare drum and, as the rimshot echoed away into the hall, he yelled, "We're gonna teach you to rock!"

It was the title of the first song and before Buddy knew what he was doing, he had jumped up the steps, run across the stage to the mike, and begun singing the opening lines. The roar of the band behind him was ear-splitting and he could hardly hear himself sing, but he hooked on to the drumbeat and the throb of the bass and let himself go. He knew it was all a bit ragged but Glenn was pounding the drums like mad and the atmosphere was electric.

By the end of the second number Mike and Jason had got the sound level right and Glenn was holding back on the noise without losing an ounce of energy and drive. They were playing well and nearly everybody in the hall was up and dancing. Even on the slow numbers nobody left the floor, though more and more people were beginning to crowd round the front of the stage to jump up and down and watch the group playing.

By halfway through the evening the front row was full of girls. During the last song before the interval Jason got down on his knees and teased them by pushing his bass towards them. One girl actually screamed and tried to grab him and he had to scramble away. As he got to his feet there was a look of shocked delight on his face. He winked at Buddy and started to dance round, faster and faster, while the song soared to the end. On the last note he and Buddy both leapt into the air and touched down perfectly as Glenn hit the final shot on the drums. The crowd at the front threw up their arms and roared. The lights went out and the curtains were drawn.

Out in the dressing room they jumped around, laughing and hugging each other in triumph. Luckily, they'd all thought of bringing a change of clothes because they were streaming with sweat. They'd just got changed when the Youth Leader came in with drinks. They gulped eagerly at the bottles while he told them how well it was going and even offered them another booking in six weeks' time.

It was hard work to start again after the break and, for a couple of numbers, the crowd was rather cool, but a burst of rock 'n' roll got them on their feet again. Even their own songs went well and Buddy was pleased with the cheers they got for 'Torn In Half'. By the end, the crowd was packed tight around the stage again and he looked down on to a heaving mass of bobbing heads and waving arms. When the curtain closed after the last song, there was a loud stamping and cries of, "More!" They wanted to sing another song but the Youth Leader held the curtains closed and pointed to his watch.

It was an anti-climax, and when they trooped off stage and slumped to the floor, the cool air of the room making them aware of their sweat-stained clothes, they all suddenly felt drained. They stayed there, not speaking, as the noise of the crowd faded and the hall emptied. At last Mike stood up slowly and wiped his face on a towel. "Well, we'd better clear up."

When they opened the doors to haul their equipment out, there were three girls waiting. They giggled, then two of them pushed the smallest one forward. She held out a pen and a piece of paper and asked for their autographs. The twins and Buddy were too amazed to move, but Glenn took it all in his stride.

"'Course you can 'ave me autograph, darling." he said, turning the girl round and putting the paper up against her back. He signed his name then added two large kisses underneath. When they had all signed the paper, the other girls came forward and asked for autographs, too.

"There you go, girls," Glenn said when they finished. "See you next time – we're back in six weeks. Tell all your mates. 'Night."

Buddy picked up his guitar to go but Glenn held his arm and whispered, "Hold on." Then he said out loud, "'Night, girls!" and waved them away. The girls giggled as they strolled off. When they had disappeared around the corner, Glenn let go of Buddy's arm.

"What was that about?" Buddy asked.

"Image, son, image. Didn't want them to see our transport, did we?"

As they carried their equipment round to the side of the hall and piled it on to Glenn's milk-float, Buddy saw what he meant.

"Superstars on a milk-float," Glenn called when they crowded into the cab with him. "We're the cream."

They began to laugh and each time they hit a bump, the empty crates rattled behind them and it all seemed funnier and funnier.

They drove through the city centre and people stared at them as they whooped and screamed with uncontrollable laughter.

Buddy hadn't said a word about 'The Reflections' to his mum and dad. He wasn't sure why he'd kept it secret but, when he thought about it, that was exactly what it was – a secret. It was something in his life, the very first thing, that he didn't want to share with them. He was doing it on his own and he didn't even want them to know about it – not yet anyway.

Whenever his dad talked about his future or about finding another group Buddy kept quiet. He lived in fear that there might be a booking for 'The Hi-Tone Four' on the same evening as he had one for 'The Reflections', but as long as it didn't happen he was happy to go on playing at the occasional wedding reception. His dad worked hard to get them bookings and he even got a gig at a pub in a nearby town for a Teddy Boy reunion evening.

"They're all mad music fans," he told Buddy, "so they'll love you. There's a couple of other groups but you lot are top of the bill. It'll be great."

It should have been great, but it was a disaster.

By the time they arrived, the pub was packed with Teddy Boys all dressed up for an evening out. The second group was just coming to the end of their set and the noise in the pub was incredible. Nobody seemed to be listening to the music; instead, there was a lot of pushing and shouting, and a feeling of violence in the air. Most of the Teddy Boys were old and fat and looked a bit pathetic with their stomachs bulging under their drape jackets. Buddy was surprised, though, to see quite a number of young people about his age. They, too, were dressed in the full Teddy Boy outfit and they seemed to be the ones who were causing most of the trouble, shoving each other around and looking as if all they wanted to do was fight.

When the second group finished, they quickly set up their equipment on the tiny stage in the corner. The pub was obviously a regular rendezvous for Teds because the juke-box was filled with old rock 'n' roll records, and while they were getting ready Buddy was horrified to hear two of the songs that he and the group were going to play.

"We can't sing those," he said to Paul, as they started to tune up. "We'll sound awful after the record."

"Nah, it'll be all right," Paul said. "OK, boys, ready?"

Paul waited for the song to stop on the juke-box then he stepped forward to the mike. "Right, boys and girls, time for some live music. I'd like to introduce 'The Hi-Tone Four' with our young vocalist, Buddy Clark."

He stomped out the beat and they launched into 'Good Golly Miss Molly'. The stage was so tiny that Buddy had to squeeze past Paul to get to the mike and by the time he got there he had missed the first line of the song. He came in on the second line and tried to put everything into his singing. Usually the lights on stage meant that he couldn't see the audience, but there were no lights here and he gazed out on a mass of bored faces. His heart sank but he kept going, trying to put as much energy as possible into it. Then, booming in louder than the group, came the sound of the original version of the song by Little Richard. Somebody had put it on the juke-box.

There was a stir in the crowd as people looked round at the juke-box, then back at the group. What with the noise of the record in front and the noise of the band behind him, Buddy couldn't hear anything else but he could see by the jeering faces that everybody was laughing. He reached the end of a verse and stepped back as Paul moved in, blowing his sax as loudly as he could to drown out the record, but it was no good.

Then Buddy saw his dad striding towards the juke-box, his face determined and angry. He bent down and pulled the plug out of the socket. The record stopped and the fight started.

One of the young boys pushed his dad aside to try to get to the plug, his dad pushed back and the next moment there was the sound of smashing glass as people dropped their beers and piled into each other. His dad disappeared behind a mob of punching, jostling Teds. Buddy stopped playing and was about to jump off the stage to go to his dad when Barry grabbed him.

"Don't be nuts – they'll tear you to pieces," he yelled.

“My dad,” Buddy yelled back but Barry kept tight hold of him and pushed him off the stage, out of the door, and on to the pavement.

Buddy struggled to get free but his guitar got in the way and Barry pinned him up against the wall. The door opened and the rest of the group ran out, carrying their instruments and amplifiers. Ernie had only managed to bring two of his drums and he dived back inside to get the third. The sounds of shouts and groans grew louder and, in desperation, Buddy ducked out of Barry’s grasp and ran to the door. Just as he reached it, Ernie came out with the third drum and, right on his heels, came Buddy’s dad with a huge grin on his face.

“Let’s split,” his dad shouted and dived into the van. The group piled their gear into the back and in less than half a minute they were screaming off down the road.

“A bundle!” his dad laughed. “Ain’t ’ad a good bundle for years.” He laughed again and honked the horn in delight.

“Are you OK, though?” Buddy asked.

“’Course I’m OK – but a couple of that lot back there will ’ave a few bumps on their mugs when they wake up tomorrow. What a laugh!”

Paul and the rest of the group didn’t think it was very funny, though, and they told him that they weren’t ever going to play a Teddy Boy gig again.

“I dunno,” his dad said, as they stood outside the breakers yard watching the group drive away. “I reckon we’re gonna ’ave to give that lot of pensioners the elbow pretty soon. They’re too old for this game. They’re all right for weddings and stuff, but they ain’t got what it takes to go on the road. What we need to find is some young blood. What do you say?”

Buddy didn’t say anything.

Despite what he’d said, his dad still announced the next day that he’d arranged for the group to play at another wedding in a week’s time. Luckily, it didn’t clash with any of the dates that ‘The Reflections’ had fixed up at other youth clubs in the area, thanks to the success of their first gig.

It was an exciting time. Even school wasn't going badly now that he had the twins as friends. The only thing that he felt he needed to make him completely happy was for his parents to get back together. Sometimes he tried to draw the conversation round to it but both of them always changed the subject, so he was just left with his hopes.

Then, in the space of three days, all his hopes were shattered.

19

On the Thursday evening before the wedding gig, Buddy decided to try out a couple of new songs. He was up in his room practising when his mum came home. She called to him and he went down to see her. The front door was open, and she hadn't taken her coat off.

"Thank God you look reasonable," she said breathlessly, looking at his clothes. "Come on – we're going out for a meal."

He picked up his jacket and followed her as she dashed out. He was halfway down the steps when he saw the parked car and the man standing beside it. His stomach lurched as he guessed who it was, but it was too late to stop.

"Buddy," his mum said, "I'd like you to meet Adrian, my boss."

"Hello," Adrian said, holding out his hand. "I've heard all about you from your mother."

Buddy took an instant dislike to the man's broad, confident face, his crinkly, well-brushed hair, and his smooth manner. He shook his hand and noticed the thick gold bracelet that slid out from the sleeve of his camel overcoat.

"Jump in," Adrian said. "I booked the table for eight o'clock."

The big car purred through the streets of the estate then headed out towards the country.

"It's rather a long way," Adrian said, "but the cuisine is superb."

The restaurant made Buddy feel awkward and uneasy. The menu was written in French and the waiters hovered around all the time, filling the glasses with wine and even grinding the pepper on to the food from a huge pepper-pot. The food was very good but he had completely lost his appetite, and he had to force himself to eat. His mum was nervous, too, and he noticed that, like him, she waited until Adrian started to eat before she was sure which knife and fork to use.

Adrian, though, was totally at home, leaning back in his chair and chatting easily about the various countries he'd visited, the people he'd met, and the unusual food he had eaten. Buddy didn't pay much attention but he could see that his mum was very impressed. She sat there, smiling and nodding, hardly able to take her eyes off her boss.

As the evening wore on, Buddy grew to dislike Adrian Mandell more and more, though he knew it wasn't really fair. There was nothing horrible about him, even if he did boast a bit. He tried hard to include Buddy in the conversation by asking about school and music and he didn't seem offended when he only got short, unfriendly answers. If anything, it was his mum who annoyed him more. She kept using her 'posh' voice and saying the sort of things she never normally said, but Buddy felt it was all Adrian's fault. Then at the end of the meal Adrian did something that made him furious.

He was talking about work and how busy things were at the office when he suddenly turned to Buddy and said, "I'd be lost without your mother, you know. She practically runs the place for me."

It wasn't what he said, it was the fact that he reached over and stroked her hand as he said it.

"I want to go – I'm tired," Buddy snapped rudely.

His mum gave him an angry look, but he didn't care.

"Yes, well, it is getting on, I suppose," Adrian said smoothly and immediately called the waiter over.

He paid the bill and they drove home in silence. As soon as the car stopped, Buddy got out without a word and ran indoors. He was already upstairs undressing when his mum came in.

"I hope you're ashamed of yourself," she said.

"No. Are you?" he said, pulling off his jeans and throwing them on the floor. He undid his shirt and put his pyjama top on. He didn't want to take his pants off in front of her but she didn't go, so he sat on the bed and stared at his feet.

"I've got nothing to be ashamed of," she said at last.

"Is he married?"

"Yes, but he's split up with his wife." There was a pause, then she added spitefully, "Split up – like me."

She swept out of the room and he had to fight hard not to howl in misery.

Luckily he had a rehearsal with 'The Hi-Tone Four' on the Friday evening, so he hardly saw his mum that day. While they were rehearsing his dad popped into the shed to watch them play. He was in a lively mood but that only made Buddy feel worse.

"Cheer up, mate, it might never 'appen," his dad said. "What's up wiv you?"

Buddy smiled and said he was fine. It wouldn't be fair to tell him because there was nothing he would be able to do about it.

The next morning he helped his mum clean the house as he usually did on Saturdays. Neither of them mentioned Adrian and they spoke nicely to each other but the whole atmosphere was strained – almost over-polite – and he was pleased when the work was done and he could leave to go and meet his dad for the wedding.

Again, his dad was in high spirits although he was disappointed that the fee they were getting for videoing the wedding and providing the evening's entertainment was very low.

"Still," he said as he and Buddy waited for the bride and groom to come out of the church, "the money may not be good, but we're both getting experience, eh? You wiv the group and me wiv the video. It all counts. 'Ello, 'ere comes the 'appy couple. Poor mugs – they'll soon be at each others' throats."

Buddy stepped back as his dad began to film again. Well, if that was what he thought about marriage, there wouldn't be much chance of him going back even if Adrian Mandell wasn't around.

The wedding reception was in a big room at a hotel, and while he was waiting to sing, Buddy stood in the kitchen looking out through the serving-hatch. He couldn't help smiling as he watched his dad moving round the tables filming the guests. Wherever he went he obviously cracked jokes because people laughed and offered him drinks. There was no doubt about it, he certainly knew how to make people happy and relaxed while he videoed them, and everyone was always pleased with the results.

There was a small, dark-haired woman dancing by herself in the middle of the floor. She had either had too much to drink or simply loved dancing because she was moving round wildly with her arms in the air and her hair swinging out round her head. His dad noticed her and, with his camera to his eye, made his way towards her through the dancing couples. She was so lost in what she was doing that she didn't notice him until he was nearly up to her. Then, as she saw him, she raised her hands, swept her hair behind her neck, and gave the camera a lovely smile.

The song ended and Paul announced Buddy. He strapped on his guitar, opened the door from the kitchen, and stepped on to the raised blocks that had been put there as a stage. All the playing he had done with the two groups had given him confidence and, although he still had a slight flutter of fear before be began, he loved singing and lost all sense of time while he was doing it.

The set went well and for the whole of the forty-five minutes, the floor was packed with dancers. Normally people danced separately, in a large group of moving bodies, so that it was impossible to tell who was dancing with whom, but during the last number he became aware of a couple jiving – holding each others' hands and whirling round together. When he looked closer, he saw that it was his dad and the woman he'd been filming. They were jiving so well that some people actually stopped dancing and stood back to watch. Buddy was glad his dad was having fun and he didn't think about it anymore until the end of the evening.

"Great gig, weren't it?" his dad said as they carried out their equipment. They put it in the back of the truck and moved towards the cab. Buddy opened the passenger door and saw the dark shape of someone sitting in the middle of the seat.

"This is Dawn," his dad said, "I'm giving 'er a lift. I'll drop you off first. Dawn – this is me kid, Buddy."

"Hello, Buddy," Dawn said as he slid on to the seat next to her. "You ain't half a great singer."

"Thanks," he mumbled, and caught the sweet, rich smell of her perfume.

"Yeah, danced our socks off, didn't we, Dawn?" his dad laughed and gunned the motor.

He drove fast and in less than ten minutes they were outside Buddy's house. He got out, said goodnight, and watched the truck roar off down the road.

The following morning he got up early and went round to the breakers yard. He did it deliberately, half-expecting what he was going to find, but it still hurt when he opened the caravan door and stepped inside. His dad was sitting up in bed and Dawn, dressed in one of his shirts, was standing at the cooker frying eggs.

"Buddy!" his dad shouted, breaking into a big smile. "You're just in time for breakfast."

"Hello, son," Dawn said, turning round and beaming at him. "Fancy some eggs? I'll put some more on."

He glared at her and stepped out of the caravan.

"Buddy," his dad called. "Where are you going?"

Buddy looked straight at Dawn and said, "I'm not your son – don't ever forget it."

He walked fast and had just turned into his street when he heard the sound of tyres screaming round the corner. He stopped and the truck drew up beside him. His dad leaned out of the window.

"Buddy? Oh come on, mate."

His dad tried a smile then looked away in confusion as Buddy stared back coldly. He hit the steering wheel softly then leaned out of the window again.

"She's dead nice," he said. "You'll like 'er. Honest."

"No, I won't."

"Oh well, 'ave it your way," he said and reached for the gearstick.

That was typical of him. He'd slip the truck into gear and just drive away from it all. Like always. He'd go away and not care how much it hurt to see him go.

Buddy moved close to the truck and said, "I don't blame you . . ."

His dad started to smile but Buddy pointed towards his house in the distance and hit him with the rest of the sentence. "After all, if she goes out with Adrian Mandell, why shouldn't you go out with Dawn?"

A glazed look came across his dad's eyes as he tried to take in the news, but Buddy didn't wait. He walked quickly to his house. As he reached the top of the steps and put the key in the lock, he saw the truck still there, his dad slumped forward with his head on the steering wheel.

For the rest of the weekend his mum looked sad. He knew that she wanted to talk to him but he didn't give her a chance. She was hurt, but he didn't care. He knew that his dad would be hurt when he didn't go round to see him on the Monday evening, but he didn't care.

Then, at school on the Tuesday, he started to feel bad, as if all the nastiness he had turned on them was suddenly bouncing back on him. He was unhappy because he had made them unhappy. Part of him wanted to go on, to twist the knife in the wound, but another part knew that the resentment was making himself miserable, too.

On the way home he bought some food and prepared a meal for his mum on her return from work. She was surprised, and it was obvious by the way she chattered away during the meal that she felt as if everything was better between them. He was glad he had made the gesture but he didn't want to give her the chance to start talking about Adrian so, at the end of the meal, he told her he was going round to see his dad. The disappointment showed in her eyes, but he ignored it and went.

All the way to the breakers yard he prayed that Dawn wouldn't be there and he was relieved to find his dad alone, slumped on a bunk watching the telly. His face lit up with pleasure, but Buddy pretended he didn't notice. He sat down on the other bunk and stared grimly at the screen.

"Buddy," his dad finally blurted out, when the ads came on, "was it true what you said the other day?"

"What?" he asked, forcing him to say it out loud.

"You know – about your mum . . . and him?"

He waited a moment, enjoying his dad's pain, then nodded briefly and looked back at the screen.

He might have known that his dad wouldn't take it lying down, but he was still stung by the reaction.

"Good," his dad said. "Then we both got someone, ain't we?"

Buddy didn't allow it to show, but the pain ripped through his chest to his heart and if he had been alone he would have burst into tears. As it was, he clamped his jaws together and continued to stare at the screen. It exploded inside him that he hated his dad, and he was grateful that a few minutes later he had a chance to let the whole of his hatred out.

"By the way," his dad announced, "I've fixed up a gig for Friday. I've rung Paul and told him. Some support band dropped out at the Leicester Club and I've got you booked instead."

"I can't go," Buddy said coolly. "I've got something else on." It was true. 'The Reflections' had a date at a youth club. At last the clash had come, and it couldn't have come at a better time.

"Well, cancel it. This is important. The Leicester Club's good news. Half-hour spot of rock 'n' roll – just you with the band backing you."

"I can't go. I've got a gig fixed with another band." He said it quietly, taking pleasure in the confusion and hurt he saw in his dad's eyes.

"What band? Where?"

"'The Reflections' – it's a group I've formed myself. We're playing the Satellite Club on Friday. We've had it arranged for weeks so you'll just have to cancel the other one, won't you?"

He got up and left. As he closed the caravan door he glimpsed his dad sitting stunned on the bunk while the signature tune of 'News at Ten' blared out from the telly.

The feeling of pleasure lasted all the way home, but he couldn't get to sleep. He thought of his dad's pain, and the embarrassment he would have of telling the club and Paul that the gig was cancelled. Most of all, though, he thought of his broken vow. He had sworn never to do anything that would make his dad unhappy. He had sworn it to God, and he had broken his word.

It worried and saddened him all week, but on the Friday evening he was caught up with the excitement of the gig. There was one awful moment, as he stepped to the mike for the first song and thought momentarily about how he had let his dad down, but he threw himself into the music and forgot it.

That was the great thing about music, you could lose yourself in it. You let the rhythm and the noise take you away and nothing else mattered for a while.

The gig was terrific and, probably because he needed to escape so badly, Buddy sang as well as he had ever sung. He knew it and the rest of the band noticed, too. In the changing-room afterwards, Mike and Jason were in the middle of telling him how great he had been when the door opened and his dad came in. It was such a shock that Buddy leaned against the wall for support.

His dad came to the centre of the room, smiling broadly at the group. There was silence as the others wondered who he was.

"Great!" his dad said, clapping the astonished Glenn on his back. "What a drummer! What a flipping group! You was all fantastic. You, too, Buddy – I ain't never 'eard you sing so good."

They turned to him for an explanation and Buddy lifted one hand slightly and said, "It's my dad."

"That's right," his dad said and Buddy saw, as if for the first time, the power and enthusiasm he could create. "I'm Buddy's dad – Terry's the name. I was out front tonight. Buddy didn't even know. And I tell you, I ain't seen nuffin' like it since I saw Buddy Holly in '58. You was fantastic. A group like you could go right to the top but . . ." he paused dramatically, "*but* you need someone to get you there. A manager. Someone to fix you up wiv gigs, demos, record contracts – the lot. Well, I'm offering to do it. What do you say?"

The excitement and confidence in his voice was infectious and it took Jason only a moment to catch it.

"Yeah!" he said, then looked enquiringly at Mike and Glenn.

They nodded and turned to Buddy. Everything told him to say no. Everything, except that small voice that reminded him of the vow, and which told him that he had caused enough pain.

He looked at his dad's pleading eyes and said, "Yes."

20

His dad insisted that the whole thing had to be done legally, so he had contracts drawn up and the official signing took place in the caravan. Buddy was the last to sign and, as he wrote his name, he saw Des King's signature at the bottom next to his dad's.

"Why's he on it?" he asked.

His dad was struggling with a bottle of fizzy wine he'd bought for the occasion and he glanced down casually and said, "Oh, just a witness. 'Ave to get it witnessed, don't you. Right, give us your glasses. Only cheap muck, this, but we'll 'ave real champagne when your first record gets in the charts."

They raised their glasses and drank a toast to 'The Reflections'.

"Can't stand that name," his dad said, draining his glass at one go. "Sounds like a bunch of girl Soul singers. You ought to 'ave something more like Buddy Holly's group, The Crickets. Animal names are always good. Look at The Beatles – they started off as The Silver Beetles."

"What about 'The Fleas'?" Buddy suggested sarcastically, feeling embarrassed at the way he was already taking over.

His dad ignored the dig but he pointedly turned his back on him and told the others that he was going to fix a date at a recording studio to make a tape of some songs so that he could send out cassettes to clubs in order to get bookings.

"You lot are good, but you got to get experience – and quick. I've thought it all out and I'm planning a big tour during the Easter 'olidays. Then, when you've really got it together, we'll start looking for a record company."

Buddy had his doubts about all these hopeful plans, but the rest of the group talked of nothing else for days. Not long afterwards his dad announced he'd booked a studio in Etchford.

The studio had been converted from a small cinema and it wasn't nearly as exciting as they had imagined. There was a control booth at one end, with a large plate-glass window behind which the engineer sat at the recording equipment. The rest of the space was just a large, bare, sound-proofed room with a piano in one corner and six microphones standing in various places on the floor.

They had all thought that they would play a song and it would be recorded in one go, but it was much longer and more complicated than that. For a start, it took nearly two hours just to set up the mikes for the drums. Then the engineer told them he would begin by recording the rhythm section, so Jason and Glenn played through the first song on their own. They found it hard, and it took nine attempts to get it right.

By then, it was way past lunchtime. They stopped for a break and, while they ate, Glenn complained to the engineer that he didn't like playing without the rest of the band.

"That's right," his dad chipped in. "In the old days, people just went in the studio – everybody played and bang! that was it."

"Well, you can do it like that if you want, but I don't advise it," the engineer said. "This way we can record all the tracks separately then mix them together so we get the best results. We can alter the balance between the instruments, and we can pick out the best bits. So, if the singer does a great version of one line but messes up the rest, we can whip the good line out and mix it in to another take."

His dad grumbled that it sounded like cheating and that if the old way was good enough for Elvis and Buddy Holly then it ought to be good enough for 'The Reflections'. But he shut up when the engineer invited him into the control booth to watch what he did.

During the afternoon, Buddy and Jason put on headphones and, while they listened to the recording of the rhythm section, they played the guitar bits. At first they found it hard to work like this, but gradually they got used to it. Then, when all the instrumental backing had been recorded, Buddy was left on his own to record the vocal.

It felt strange, standing alone in the studio in front of the mike with the others peering at him through the glass of the control box, and he panicked. The first take was a disaster. He sang out of tune, lost the rhythm, and finally forgot the words.

"Just take it easy," the engineer said through the headphones. "We've got lots of time, and remember we can pick out bits from each take, so relax and enjoy yourself."

"OK," Buddy said. "But can you turn the headphones up real loud?"

"Anything you want," came the reply. "Here we go, then. Take two."

The music came blasting into his ears so loud that it almost hurt, but he didn't mind. He closed his eyes, leaned towards the mike and began to sing. It was a perfect take and when he finished he could hear the excited chatter from the control box.

"That was great," the engineer said, "but let's just do one more for luck. Ready? Take three . . ."

The third take was just as good and they moved on to the next song. They were all getting used to having to play and sing separately, but it was still a slow process to record all the various tracks and it was after three o'clock in the morning before they finished the third and final song.

They were exhausted as they bundled into the truck for the drive home, but his dad was high with energy and talked non-stop about the various recording techniques he'd learned and how fantastic modern studios were.

"Thought you preferred the old way of doing it," Buddy said, irritated by the way his dad was pretending to know so much.

"Nah, never said that – all I said was Elvis and them others done OK like that. But you gotta move wiv the times, ain't you!"

Four days later his dad went over to the studio and picked up the finished tape and the fifty copies he'd ordered. They crowded in to the caravan to listen and they had to agree that the tape was good. They weren't the best performances they'd ever given but, as his dad said, they were certainly good enough to show people what the group was like.

"You see, when I send these cassettes off, the offers'll come pouring in."

They didn't exactly pour in, but by the end of the term they had fourteen dates fixed up for what his dad kept grandly calling 'The Easter Tour'. The gigs were all in pubs and clubs and were limited to within a radius of a hundred miles because Glenn and his dad still had to work during the days. They rehearsed hard then spent the evenings at the caravan making plans. Then, one day, his dad proudly pointed to a pile of leaflets he had got printed.

"Publicity," he said, handing copies round. "We'll give 'em out wherever we go. It's got a list of dates and a bit of writing about each of you."

"Here, Terry, what's this?" Mike asked.

Buddy looked down and saw the heading: 'Easter Tour – Buddy and the Bosses'.

"Oh yeah, I've changed the name," his dad said calmly. "Never liked the other one. This is miles better – makes you sound tougher, a bit mean-like. I thought of 'Buddy and the Guvnors' but it weren't as good. This is the one that's gonna sell you. I put me life on it."

Buddy felt terrible but his dad kept saying how great the name was and in the end he persuaded them to accept it. Nevertheless, Mike said that in future any big decision should only be made after they had all voted on it.

When he walked to school on the last morning of term, Buddy was just about to cross a road in the centre of town when he was astonished to see the name of the group written in big purple letters on a wall opposite. As soon as he got into the common room he was met by the twins who had seen the name sprayed across two posters.

"We thought it might've been you," Jason said, "but it must've been Glenn."

Buddy shook his head. "It wasn't Glenn. There's only one person mad enough to do that – my dad."

The twins thought it was a laugh and said it was great that they'd got a manager who would try anything to help the group, but Buddy was furious at what was going on. All his worst fears about having his dad as manager were coming true. He was ready to have a row about it, but when he went round to the caravan that evening and saw his dad's hands and jeans stained with purple paint, he couldn't help laughing.

"Honestly, Dad, you're nuts," he said, trying to sound angry.

"'Ave you seen 'em?" his dad grinned. "Took me 'alf the night. I used five cans of paint. Ruined me jeans – look at them! Still, it's worth it. The whole town'll 'ave the name in their 'eads in a week's time. Honest, mate – I can't tell you what the group means to me. The morning I got out of nick, the Governor called me in – dead sarky, 'e was – said 'e hoped 'e wouldn't see me back too soon. They all think I can't do nuffin'. Your mum, too. Well – I'll show 'em."

Sometimes his dad could be the worst liar Buddy knew – swearing black was white, if it suited him. At other times, no one ever talked to him so truthfully, opened themselves so nakedly, and showed what they really felt. Most of the time, Buddy felt like a stranger in the world, as if he didn't fit, and that all the people round him had emotions and thoughts that weren't like his. Then his dad would say something so honest and so straight that he knew he wasn't alone.

They spent the evening listening to music and his dad got out a map and showed him the route they would take to get to the first gig the next day.

As he folded the map away, he suddenly asked, "Buddy, do you mind if Dawn comes wiv us tomorrow? She's found someone to look after her kids."

Did he mind? He'd half-thought his dad would bring her, but he hadn't expected him to ask, and the question had caught him by surprise. Over the past month she had often been at the caravan and she'd always been nice to him, even when he hadn't been very friendly to her. It wasn't fair to expect his dad to live a lonely life, but it still hurt to see him with Dawn. She was fifteen years younger than him, for a start – but that wasn't the real reason. While she was around, there was no chance that his dad would come home and, deep in his heart, that was what he hoped for.

"Well, do you mind?" his dad asked again.

Buddy nodded.

"Why? She's a sweet kid, you know – and she really likes you."

"I know."

"Why then?"

Buddy shrugged. "I don't know – it just makes me sad, that's all."

His dad looked directly at him for a moment then put his elbows on his knees and bent his head, running his hands through his hair. "Oh Gawd, Buddy – I never wanna make you sad but . . . Cor, what a mess. OK, then, I'll tell 'er there ain't enough room in the truck. She'll understand."

It was the first chance he'd had to talk seriously with his dad, and he couldn't stop now. "Do you love her?"

"Dawn?" his dad lifted his head and stared at the table as if he was thinking about it for the first time. "I like 'er – a lot. She's a bit scatterbrained but she's got a heart of gold and she makes me laugh. And I need a laugh sometimes living in this place." He paused and rubbed his forehead. "But I don't love 'er – no. I've only ever loved one woman, but I ain't good enough for 'er now. You saw what it was like. Is she still seeing that bloke?"

"Don't know. He hasn't been round the house again, but she stays out late sometimes. We don't talk about it."

His dad nodded. "Oh well, you'd better go 'ome and get some sleep. Big day tomorrow."

The tour didn't start very well. It was a long journey and, despite all his preparations, his dad got lost when they arrived in the town. They drove round and round, stopping to ask, but nobody knew where the club was. When they finally found it, hidden away in the basement of a large building next to a derelict factory, they only had half an hour before the doors opened. They set up their equipment fast, made a quick soundcheck, then changed in a dingy little room behind the stage. As he unfolded his shirt, Buddy found a good-luck card his mum had slipped inside it.

They had known that they were booked as the support band to start the evening, but it had never occurred to them that most people would only turn up later. As it was, there were less than thirty in the audience when they began to play. Even these people had obviously only come to see the main band and they spent most of the time talking at the bar, hardly paying any attention to the music. His dad tried to get some applause going after the first couple of songs but, when no one joined in, even he stopped.

By the time they got to the last song, the audience had grown much larger and some people had started to dance, but it was too late to show them what they could do. While they packed their gear, Buddy saw his dad handing out leaflets, but most people just dropped them on the floor.

The only good moment was when they were loading their equipment on to the truck. The club's manager came out with their money and as he handed the envelope to his dad, he said, "Good little band you got there. We'll have them back sometime."

It wasn't enough to cheer them up, though, and they were all very quiet on the long journey home. They were even more fed-up when they got back and his dad worked out what they had made. After expenses, there was hardly a couple of quid each.

"Won't keep me in guitar strings, that won't," Mike said.

His dad looked at their long faces and groaned. "Blimey, what a load of wallies. Get it through them thick nuts of yours – it ain't gonna be roses all the way. You gotta get known and that's gonna be flipping 'ard work."

It *was* hard work. In the next eighteen days they drove over two thousand miles in the crowded and uncomfortable cab of the truck. They played thirteen gigs, always as support band and usually to small audiences who didn't seem to care what they did. They humped their equipment in and out of pubs and clubs, often having to change their clothes in smelly lavatories. They all caught colds but had to keep going even when they felt so rotten they just wanted to stay in bed and sleep.

It was worse for Glenn because he also had to do his milk-round, and he found it terribly hard to get up in the morning when they'd come home late the night before. He often slept through the journeys, snoring loudly with his head on someone's shoulder, yet he always came alive whenever they were on stage – pounding his drums wildly as if he had energy to spare. He was getting better, too, sometimes trying out intricate new rhythms in the middle of a song. In fact, they were all getting better, and by the end of the tour Buddy knew that they were playing really well.

Luckily, on their last gig they had a chance to show how good they'd become. It was at a pub and although they were the support band and had only been booked for a forty-five minute spot, the room was already packed when they started, and the whole atmosphere was different. From their first song, Buddy felt the crowd was with them and there was loud applause after each number – unlike the silence they usually faced. Their whole performance was lifted and, when they reached the end of their set, the audience wouldn't let them go. They played four encores and the crowd was still shouting for more when they left the stage.

The leader of the other band scowled at them as they went into the changing room, buzzing with excitement from the reaction they'd got.

"You were supposed to have finished twenty-five minutes ago," he said.

"Yeah, sorry," Mike said, "but they wanted more."

"I don't care what they wanted. We're the lead group round here, not you amateurs."

The man was squaring up to Mike, and for a moment it looked as if there might be a fight. Then his dad's voice came from the doorway.

"Got a problem, mush?" He put down the bottle and glasses he was carrying and walked quickly over to the man. "Rattled by the competition, are you? Yeah, well why don't you get out on stage and see if you can do as good? Or are you worried you can't follow them?"

The man stared at his dad but it was obvious he didn't dare start anything with him and after a second he turned to his group and said, "Come on, lads, let's go."

As soon as they had filed out, his dad picked up the bottle and said, "OK, you lot, I promised you champagne for your first hit but you were so damn good tonight I thought we'd 'ave some now."

He poured the champagne and then raised his glass. "Well, it's bin 'ard work but you ain't 'alf done well. I'm proud of you. You've stuck together when it weren't easy – and that's a good sign. You've played well. You've learned a lot and now, the next fing we gotta do is see about getting you on record."

21

It was hard to settle back into the routine of school after the tour but luckily they still had the local Youth Club dates to keep them going. Each time they played they began to see the same faces in the audience, and it was obvious that they were building up a reputation in the town. His dad claimed it was because of all the notices he had painted on walls and posters, and the fact that he made sure the gigs were always announced on the local radio station. It was true that he worked hard on publicity. He had some more leaflets run off and spent a couple of Saturdays handing them out to young people in the shopping centre. Then he arranged for a reporter from the local paper to interview them and review one of their gigs.

The following week they rushed out to buy the paper, and found they were on the centre page. The article made Buddy cringe because it was full of lies that his dad had told the reporter about how they were negotiating a contract with a big record company and how they'd been booked to appear on TV, but the review was very good. The reporter said that they were 'an excellent young group' and that their show was 'the most exciting' he had seen for a long time. There was a large photo of them, the photographer having managed to catch Buddy and Jason as they leaped into the air at the end of a song. It looked great, so Buddy cut it out and pinned it on his bedroom wall.

The thing that most pleased his dad was the headline: 'Buddy and the Bosses in Business'.

"There you are," he said. "I told you it was an ace name. Papers love names they can play around wiv."

"Yeah," said Jason, "it'll be 'Buddy and the Bosses on the Dole' if they find out about the lies you told them."

"That's not lying – that's publicity, son. Papers don't care what they print as long as it's interesting."

Buddy didn't really agree with his dad's attitude, but he had to admit that the publicity worked. At their next gig there was a big queue outside when they arrived, and by the time the show began the hall was so full that latecomers were turned away. People at school started to talk to him and the twins about the group, and even the headmistress stopped them in the corridor one day and asked if they would play a concert at the end of term for the leavers.

Glenn said that a lot of people on his milk-round recognized him and asked about the group, and that quite a number of his friends were fans.

"It's a great way to pull the birds, too," he grinned. "I've been out with three different chicks this week alone. Gotta admit it, kids, I'm the sex symbol of this outfit!"

It was true that Glenn was the one who got asked for the most autographs after gigs and he usually ended up scribbling down the names and addresses of the prettiest girls. Buddy, though, had noticed two girls who turned up at all the gigs and stood right in front of the mike looking up at him while he sang, and one day he found them waiting outside his house when he got home from school. He signed autographs for them, then went inside.

About half an hour later he happened to glance out of the window and they were still there, so he went out and talked to them. They were both fifteen and they told him they'd bunked off their last lesson in order to be there when he got home. He was flattered but it wasn't very easy to talk to them because they kept giggling. He was just about to go inside when one of them shoved a letter into his hand and the two of them ran off down the road. He waited until he got inside, then tore the envelope open. Written on a piece of pink notepaper was the message:

> 'I love you. If you would like to go out with me meet me tomorrow at the clock-tower at 7.30. Elaine.'

She had scrawled seventeen kisses after her name. He counted every one of them.

Despite the fact that it was quite warm the following evening, he decided to wear the long black overcoat he had bought at a second-hand shop. His mum said it made him look like an out-of-work gangster, but he thought he looked great in it and he kept sneaking glances at his reflection in the shop windows he passed.

He was nearly at the clock-tower when an awful thought hit him – supposing Elaine wasn't the girl who'd given him the letter. She was pretty, with big brown eyes and long curly hair, but the other one had short greasy hair and a mouth that was sulky and miserable. He stopped at the corner and hid in a shop doorway, peering out at the clock-tower. At exactly seven-thirty a girl in a white mac ran across the road and looked up at the clock – it was the pretty one.

"Hi," he said as he reached her.

"Hello," she said. "Doreen bet me you wouldn't come."

"Is Doreen your friend? Well, I did, didn't I – so she owes you some money. What do you want to do?"

She giggled and took hold of his hand. Her hand was cool and clammy but he held on while they crossed the road, then he let go and put his arm round her shoulder. It was the first time he had held a girl close and his heart was pounding fast. As they walked up the street he hoped they would meet someone he knew so that they would see him with a girl.

"Do you fancy the pictures?" he asked.

"OK."

It was ridiculous, but it even gave him a thrill to hand the money over and ask for two tickets. The usherette showed them into the back row and he couldn't help wondering if it was because they looked like people in love. As soon as they sat down Elaine took his hand again and, despite the clamminess, he didn't want to let go. He wished he'd taken his coat off though. It was hot in the cinema and he might start sweating.

At last the lights began to dim. Elaine squeezed his hand and, as the curtains opened, she leaned round in front of his face and kissed him. She pushed him back into the seat, slid her arms round his neck, stroked his hair and crushed her lips against his. Her mouth tasted sweet and minty and there was a surge through his body that made his chest feel as if it would explode with excitement.

He saw hardly any of the film and as they left the cinema he glanced quickly at the photos outside in case his mum asked him what it had been about. They walked back to Elaine's house and again he caught himself wishing someone would see them together. He felt wonderful and even the drizzle sweeping into their faces on the warm blustery wind seemed romantic. They huddled together on Elaine's doorstep and kissed until there was a knock from the front window. It was her mother, and they immediately broke apart.

"Can I see you tomorrow?" he asked as Elaine opened the door.

"OK."

"Same place, same time," he said, and was aware of how many times he had heard lovers say it in films.

Buddy felt so good he could hardly stop himself from running and singing on the way home. His mum looked at him strangely as he got in and when he saw himself in the bathroom mirror he knew why. His lips were swollen and the skin round his mouth was red and sore. He got into bed, worrying that he had caught some awful disease from Elaine and it drove all other thoughts of her out of his mind.

The next morning, though, he was relieved to find that his mouth was back to normal and he started looking forward to seeing her again. That evening was fine and they walked along the sea-front and up on to the cliffs to watch the sun going down. They sat on a bench, sheltered from the breeze by a gorse bush. Buddy wanted to talk to her. He imagined being able to tell her all the things about himself that he'd never told anyone, but he didn't get the chance. All Elaine wanted to do was kiss. It excited him, of course, but he wished they could sometimes stop long enough to talk a bit. He tried to start a conversation as they walked back to town but she didn't seem very interested, so he couldn't bring himself to tell her anything important. It was great just being with a girl, though, and he told himself he was in love and that it would last forever.

It lasted one week.

On the eighth evening she didn't turn up at the clock-tower. He waited for ages then went round to her house and stood outside, trying to pluck up the courage to ring the bell, but he didn't.

He missed her terribly and his mum noticed how miserable he was but he told her it was nothing. He thought of writing and asking what had happened but he tore up the letter he wrote. Eventually he told Jason about it. Jason just laughed and said she'd probably been put off by his bad breath. It was only a joke but Buddy couldn't help cupping his hand over his mouth every so often during the next few days and sniffing to see if it was true.

Then, at their next gig, Elaine and her friend, Doreen, were there in the front row. He smiled at her in delight and kept looking at her when he sang. He even dedicated one of the love songs to 'someone special' and looked straight at her when he said it. Afterwards, she was hanging around outside the hall and he asked her why she hadn't kept the date. All the way through the gig he had been imagining that she would tell him that her parents had stopped her seeing him, but she just said that she didn't want to get serious.

"Doreen would like to go out with you, though," she said.

He told her to get lost and went and sat in the truck while the others loaded the gear in the back.

"Who's that bird you was talking to?" his dad asked.

"Just some silly groupie," he said, hating her.

"Yeah, well watch yourself – OK? Don't want you getting involved wiv the first bit of stuff that comes along."

"You can talk," he snapped spitefully, and his dad gave him a dirty look and was just about to say something when the others opened the door and got into the cab with them.

That gig was the last one they had arranged in the area and although a number of Youth Clubs wanted them back, his dad turned them down.

"Don't want to let 'em get fed up wiv you," he explained. "Anyway, I've got it all planned. I'm gonna send out more cassettes and fix up a whole week of bookings for your 'alf-term. London, this time, and a few of the bigger cities down West. Then we'll go back in the studio and record a couple of songs and I'll get 'em pressed up as a single. I'll send copies off to the big record companies and we'll release it in the shops down 'ere and see if we can get it in the charts."

"It costs loads to make a record," Buddy pointed out.

"You worry about the music and let me worry about the cash, OK?" his dad said. "Might make a video, too. Get on the telly and send it off to the record companies. Can't get nowhere wivout videos nowadays."

Buddy thought the plans sounded a bit too ambitious, and he was also worried about where his dad was planning to raise the money, but he couldn't help being as excited as the others. He went home, anxious to tell his mum what was going to happen, but when he got in she was sitting on the sofa watching the flickering images on the telly with the sound turned off. She looked as if she had been crying. He asked her what the matter was but she shook her head and said it was nothing.

He went and made a cup of tea. As he put her cup down on the sofa she looked up at him, and he saw there were tears in her eyes.

"Adrian's handed in his notice," she said. "He's been offered a big job in London, starting September."

He could hardly keep from smiling and he had to go and stand at the window so that she wouldn't see. It was great news. He didn't want her to be unhappy but she'd get over it, like he was getting over losing Elaine. Perhaps he could even tell her about all that so that she wouldn't feel so lonely. He heard her get up and walk across the room. There was a click as she switched off the silent telly, then she came to the window and put her arms round his chest and held him tight. Yes, he would tell her about Elaine – they could talk together about how sad it was to lose someone you loved.

She let go of him and walked back to the sofa and sat down.

"He wants us to go with him, Buddy. You and me. He's asked the new firm if he can take me as his assistant, and they've said yes."

The news was like a blow across his chest but somehow he managed to keep his voice level as he asked, "What did you tell him?"

"I said I'd think about it. I wanted to talk to you first."

His hand shook violently as he raised the cup to his lips. The tea was scaldingly hot but he gulped it down fast, bringing tears to his eyes. He wouldn't let her see them – she might think he was crying. He picked up the saucer and went towards the kitchen.

"Buddy, what do you think?"

He kept his voice level and calm again – almost light and uncaring – as he called back, "It's up to you, isn't it?"

22

"It's up to you," was what he said every time his mum asked him what he thought about the move.

When he was still saying it three days later, she got angry but he didn't care. She shouted at him and then started crying, but he didn't budge. If she wanted to change their lives like that, she would have to make the decision on her own – he wasn't going to help her. Of course he didn't want to go. It would probably mean the end of the group; he'd have to start a new school and a new life; but, worst of all, it would mean being separated from his dad. There was always the possibility that he could move into the caravan with him, but there wasn't really enough room and they'd be bound to get on each other's nerves. Besides, he couldn't be sure that his dad would want him now that he had Dawn. And, anyway, it would be awful to be separated from his mum if she went and he stayed.

His song, 'Torn In Half', seemed more real than ever.

After the big row, she stopped asking what he thought and that was almost worse. Day after day he expected her to tell him what she had decided and he found himself swept backwards and forwards between hope that she would stay and fear that she would go. It was as if his brain was trying to torture him. If he tried to be hopeful, he immediately started thinking of all the reasons why she would probably go.

His brain seemed like an enemy that wanted him to be unhappy. He felt split into pieces – one part of him was thinking, she'll stay; another part was thinking, she'll go; and a third part was thinking that his brain was an enemy. How could he think these things at the same time, and why couldn't he stop thinking about things that he didn't want to think about? He wasn't in charge of his brain – it was in charge of him. And if that was true, who was he? At times it felt as if he was going mad.

The only thing that could stop all these thoughts from swirling round and round in his head was music. Best of all, was getting together with the others and playing something fast and loud that drove away everything except the noise and the rhythm in his ears. When he couldn't play with the group, he played on his own – sitting in his bedroom, strumming chords and trying to make up songs about how he felt. He wrote one called 'Nothing Serious' about Elaine and what she had said, and another one called 'Brain Train' about the weird feeling that his brain controlled him.

The twins really liked 'Brain Train' and they helped him rewrite some of the verses, but Glenn said it was morbid and preferred loves songs like 'Nothing Serious'. As for his dad, he didn't like them singing anything but the old rock 'n' roll songs.

"They're all right, I suppose," he said when they played him the two new songs, "but I don't know why you bother. The old stuff always goes down a bomb."

Buddy was pleased with the songs and he hated the way his dad always put them down, but before he had a chance to say something cutting, Mike spoke.

"We'll never get anywhere without our own material, Terry. Everyone's heard those old songs a million times – they're thirty years old."

"Oldies but goodies," his dad said. "The Tower of London's thousands of years old. I suppose you'd knock it down and build a new one if you 'ad the chance."

Mike groaned and raised his eyebrows sarcastically. "Look, if we want to sing new songs as well as the old stuff, we will. Like you said, we worry about the music and you take care of the business side – bookings for instance."

His dad would have gone on arguing but the word 'bookings' shut him up because he'd got the dates of the half-term muddled up and had arranged the six gigs for a week when they were back at school. Obviously they couldn't cancel them but it was going to be hard work, especially as one of the gigs meant a two-hundred mile drive to the West Country and back the same night. Actually, Buddy was pleased about that date because it was near where Julius and Charmian Rybeero lived. He'd written to tell them about it and they'd replied, promising that they would be there to see him play. It would be good to see them again after all this time.

They rehearsed hard over the half-term because they knew that, in a way, the six gigs were going to be the most important they'd ever played. The four London dates, in particular, would be special because they might be seen by somebody from a record label or the music press.

The first London gigs, on Monday and Tuesday, were in pubs and, although they were only the support band as usual, the whole atmosphere was more exciting than other places they'd played. The pubs were packed with people who saw a lot of groups so they had to work hard to prove themselves. Buddy was very nervous but he felt charged up, and he stormed through the songs while Jason and Glenn set a driving beat, and Mike played some soaring guitar solos.

The odd thing was that at the first gig it was the old songs that got the loudest applause and his dad made a big point of telling them so on the journey home. The following evening, though, the audience definitely preferred the new songs and Mike couldn't resist rubbing it in while his dad tried to squirm out of it. Buddy had to laugh but he didn't like the way his dad and Mike were beginning to pick on each other at every opportunity.

They had to leave straight after school for the Wednesday night gig, but despite the early start they hit a lot of traffic and the first part of the two-hundred mile journey was so slow that they began to worry about being there on time. They got on to the motorway and his dad pushed the truck along at top speed so that they finally arrived with an hour to spare. They ate at a hamburger restaurant then drove to the club.

There was big queue filing through the club doors and they were thrilled to see the posters on the wall – 'Tonight: Buddy and the Bosses. Plus local support group.' While his dad took a photo of them in front of the poster Buddy kept checking the queue for Charmian and Julius. There was no sign of them, but Mike and Jason met up with their friend Dave who'd travelled up from Plymouth.

"Hi," he said to Buddy as they were introduced, "I hear you're good. Should be interesting."

It was the first time they'd had to wait before going on and it was nerve-racking sitting in the dressing-room while the local group played their set. Dave's comment had sounded like a challenge, and Buddy was extra-nervous because he wanted to do well. Apart from that, it would be terrible to make a mess of things in front of Jules and Char – if they were there.

By the time they finally got on stage, Buddy was very tense and during the first song he could feel his voice was tight and strained. Mike noticed, too, and when Buddy turned round and took a swig of Coke, he gave a worried look and asked if he was OK.

"Sure," Buddy said, and went back to the mike. He peered out at the audience and there, just in front of the stage, were the Rybeeros. They smiled and waved at him and he felt a sudden surge of confidence. He would sing for them.

"Good evening," he said into the mike. "We're 'Buddy and the Bosses'. And this second song is for a couple of old friends of mine who are out there tonight. Char,

Jules – this is for the good times we had. A-one, a-two, a-one, two, three . . ."

From then on, he gave it everything he had. His voice relaxed and, as he began to loosen up and enjoy himself, the band caught the mood and started to rock with him. By the end they were all pouring with sweat and the whole club was alive with energy and excitement.

Buddy knew it had been a good gig – perhaps the best they'd ever done, but it was still satisfying to have someone like Dave say it. He came into the dressing-room and shook Buddy's hand.

"They were right, you're terrific. The whole band was brilliant. I'd love to play with you sometime."

Before Buddy could reply, the door opened and in burst Charmian and Julius.

Char got to him first and threw her arms round him and gave him a kiss while Jules patted him on the back. It was great to see them and they started talking easily as if it were only a week since they'd last met. Char looked just the same, but Jules had shot up and was now almost six inches taller than Buddy remembered him. There was so much to talk about, but after half an hour Char said they'd have to go because their dad would be waiting.

Buddy went outside with them and found his dad leaning up against a taxi talking to Mr Rybeero.

"Hello, Buddy," Mr Rybeero said. "Your dad's been telling me you're a good singer now."

"He's great," Char said.

Buddy went over to the truck to put his guitar inside and Julius came with him.

"Blimey, I don't half envy you," Julius said, kicking the wheel of the truck. "I'd give anything to go back with you. This place is a dump."

"I thought you liked it."

"No, it's dead. Here, I bet you pull all the birds with this singing lark, don't you?"

Buddy laughed. "Not really. Have you got a girl?"

"No. Char's got some bloke, but I can't find anyone."

Julius suddenly seemed miserable and Buddy tapped him on the arm and said, "Nor can I, mate. Don't worry about it."

"Oh yeah," Julius said, "it's OK for you – nothing ever worries you."

Buddy could hardly believe it. All these years he had always thought that Jules was the one who never worried, who seemed to glide happily through life without a care; and yet here was Jules thinking the same thing about him. He looked at his old friend and didn't know how to begin telling him the truth. How could people be so wrong about each other?

"Come on, Julius," Mr Rybeero called.

"I'll write to you," Buddy said as Jules slumped into the back seat of the taxi. "'Bye, Char."

He kissed her cheek and she got in beside her brother. Mr Rybeero hooted the horn, did a U-turn, and the taxi sped away down the street.

"Right, now let's get one fing straight," his dad said as they piled into the truck. "I ain't some flipping roadie. I 'ad to load all the gear tonight while you lot was gassin' – and I ain't gonna do it on me own again. It's share and share alike."

"And where were you while we were working on stage? Propping up the bar, I expect," Mike said coldly.

His dad glared at him then rammed the truck into gear and they started on the long journey home. Glenn fell asleep immediately but Mike and Jason told Buddy how impressed Dave had been with the group.

"He offered to play keyboards with us when we make the record," Jason said. "What do you think, Terry? He's damn good."

His dad didn't reply.

He was obviously in such a bad mood that they drove the rest of the way in silence and got home just as the sun was coming up. Poor Glenn had to go straight to work but Buddy got a couple of hours' sleep – although he still nodded off during his maths lesson and was shouted at by the teacher.

By the end of the week they were all exhausted, but the final gig raised their spirits. It was in a famous club in the West End of London and, although they were first on the bill and only had a half-hour spot, it was a thrill to be standing on the stage where some of the best known bands in the world had played. It helped to inspire them and they poured all their energy into it.

The following week they got their first mention in the music papers. It was only three lines long but his dad cut it out and stuck it up on the caravan wall. They all looked at it so many times that they soon knew it by heart and every so often one of them would suddenly recite it: "Early evening blues were lifted by a bright, poppy half-hour from 'Buddy and the Bosses' – young, raw and alive. Watch out for them."

The review decided his dad that they were ready to go into the studio again. He booked a whole weekend session and then began the long discussion about which two songs they were going to record. His dad, of course, put forward two old rock 'n' roll songs, but he was outvoted and they finally chose 'Torn In Half' and 'Nothing Serious'.

They rehearsed the songs solidly for a week and a half and Buddy and Glenn thought they sounded fine but the twins kept saying how much better they'd be with Dave on keyboards. In the end they persuaded them to send for him. Buddy wasn't sure about the idea, especially as Dave couldn't join them until two days before they went into the studio. Yet, on the very first rehearsal, he realized that the twins had been right. Dave was terrific and he fitted in at once, filling out the whole sound and coming up with great ideas for the arrangement. Even his dad was impressed and they all went into the studio feeling optimistic.

Once again, the recording sessions were slow, hard and sometimes tedious work, but by the Sunday evening they had recorded and mixed the two songs. They were all tired and slightly numb from having to hear the tracks over and over for the mix, but as they listened to the finished master tape they knew that they had produced something good.

On the Monday his dad took the tape up to a London studio and four days later he went up again to fetch the discs. They were all waiting for him at the breakers yard when he got back. He jumped out of the truck, ripped open one of the cardboard boxes, and handed each of them a record.

"Hey, Terry, who did these covers? They're great," Jason said.

"Bit of class, eh?" his dad said, smiling proudly.

Buddy had expected something in plain white but his dad had taken the photo from the local paper and had it printed across the cover. It was blown up so that the black dots of the newsprint were big and grainy. Then, across the photo, in big red letters, was the name of the group.

"Dad, they're brilliant," he said.

"Yeah, but this is just the start. Now what we need is an ace video – and I'm gonna make it!"

23

It rained the entire weekend when they were supposed to make the video. Everything was set up – Dave had come from Plymouth, they had hired the Teddy Body suits they were going to wear, and the workers at the breakers yard were all ready. When the rain continued to pour down and the forecast said it would be the same the next day, they had to postpone making the video until the following weekend. His dad was so disappointed that when the others all went home, Buddy stayed in the caravan to try and cheer him up by listening as he went over the plans for the video for about the twentieth time.

They had chosen 'Torn In Half' and his dad had made up a sort of story to illustrate the song. The opening scene would show Buddy sitting in an old car that was being pushed towards the yard by the rest of the group. Once the car was inside the yard there would be scenes of the group playing while the car was pulled to pieces – first by people taking away spare parts, then by the machines that ripped it apart and finally crushed it into scrap metal. His dad had planned each shot carefully, making sure that they had plenty of close-ups of the group, although never singing.

"It's a pity about that," his dad said, "but this video bloke says it's impossible to dub the sound and get the lip movements perfect wivout really good equipment."

"Who is this bloke?"

"Oh, one of Des's mates. 'The Video King' they call 'im – runs off about a hundred pirate videos a day and makes a fortune. Anyway, 'e knows everyfing about editing so it'll be a great 'elp. Ah Gawd, I just 'ope it don't rain next week. I'll go spare."

Luckily, it turned out hot and sunny – too hot, in fact, for Buddy and the group. The Teddy Boy suits were thick and heavy so that they sweated even when they weren't doing anything, which wasn't very often. Every little section had to be filmed about ten times before his dad was satisfied, and they had to keep stopping to wipe their faces under the burning sun.

"We'll look like a load of singing beetroots," Glenn said as his dad called them for yet another take of a scene.

Although the record was going to be dubbed over the finished film by the Video King, they had a huge cassette-player set up which played the relevant bit of the song over and over while they filmed each scene until they were fed up with hearing it. Some of the sequences were very difficult to film and one of the most dangerous took them all Sunday morning to get right. The group had to sit in the almost wrecked car while it was lifted up by the crane and swung round towards the crushing machine. They were terrified each time they did it in case the crane lost its grip and the car crashed to the ground. His dad, though, was so involved with the work that he became fearless, sitting precariously on the bonnet while the crane lifted and swung them. Buddy hardly dared look because his dad, using both hands to steady the camera, couldn't hold on to anything to stop himself falling.

"Remember, I want you to look scared," his dad kept shouting at them.

It wasn't hard to do.

For ten days after that, his dad disappeared. Each time Buddy went to the caravan there was a note stuck on the door saying, 'Gone down the Video King's'. It was a useless piece of information and, after a couple of days, Buddy wrote on the paper – 'What's the address?' The question remained unanswered.

Then one day he arrived and found the door open again. His dad was sitting inside looking pale, with dark rings under his eyes, but there was nothing tired about his voice.

"Buddy!" he shouted. "'Ello, mate. Cor, what a time I've 'ad. That bloke's a flipping genius, 'e is. What 'e don't know about videos ain't worth knowing. 'E oughta be working in telly. And I've learned so much. If only I could do that film again it'd be miles better. But 'e says it's great anyway. Just wait till you see it. 'E's done wonders wiv it – all on ropey old equipment, too."

"Haven't you got it, then?"

"Nah – need a couple more days to splice it all together, then 'e'll make a master tape and run off the copies. Honest, 'e's a genius."

His dad was high with excitement and he showed him a list of things he was going to do. As soon as the video was ready he was going to send it off to the television stations to see if they could get it on one of the big music programmes. He said most stations would ignore it but that there was a good chance it might be shown on the video review that the local TV did each week. He was also going to use the video to interest the pubs and clubs in the area because he wanted the group to play as many local dates as possible when they got the record into the shops.

"We've got to make sure it gets into the charts round 'ere, then I can send a copy of it when I send the video and the disc off to the big record labels."

"Dad, we can't be sure it'll get in the charts."

"Wanna bet? I found out that the newspaper uses two shops to compile their chart. All we 'ave to do is get plenty of people to go there and buy it. And they're bound to if I give 'em the money to do it, ain't they!"

"You can't do that. Besides, we'll lose money if we buy our own record."

"It's only to get it started. Once it's in the charts, people'll buy it anyway. It's done all the time."

"But where's the money coming from?"

His dad tapped the side of his nose and Buddy knew better than to ask anymore. Anyway, he had a good idea that Des King was involved. That signature on the contract wasn't just as witness, as his dad had said. It worried him to have King and his crooked deals mixed up with it all, but there was nothing he could do.

There was no stopping his dad in the mood he was in. He called the group together one evening and fired them with enthusiasm telling them all his plans. He casually announced that he'd just come back from 'Goliath's', the big club on the sea-front, and that they had booked the group for two evenings a week for seven weeks during July and August.

"Pretty neat, eh?" he laughed. "It's the place all the 'olidaymakers go. I 'ad a job persuading them. Then I played 'em this."

He switched on the telly and pressed a button on the video machine. It was the video of 'Torn In Half' and it was stunning. All during the filming they had hoped it would turn out well but this was better than they'd ever dreamed. The music roared along while the pictures cut from one shot to another in time to the beat, and the result looked even more exciting and dangerous than it had felt to do it. They were all so amazed that it wasn't until after the third showing that they could take it in.

"I've got to hand it to you, Terry – that's fantastic," Mike said.

"Ta. But 'alf of it is down to the Video King. Now just let's 'ope we can cash in on it."

During the last week of the summer term there weren't many lessons so Buddy and the twins used the end-of-term concert as an excuse to spend most of the time rehearsing. Dave wasn't going to be able to get up to play with them at 'Goliath's' and the other gigs his dad was arranging, but Glenn came round to the school every day when he had finished his milk-round and they spent hours practising new material.

The school concert went very well and the headmistress came backstage afterwards to thank them, although she did add that their reports showed that they were all spending too much time on the music.

"Music's all very well," she said, "and, as I say, I thought this evening was super. But you'll have to put a great deal more effort into your work next year."

"Yeah, if we're still here, darling," Jason said after she had closed the door behind her.

It was great to put his school books away and look forward to seven weeks of making music, but Buddy couldn't help remembering Jason's comment. Perhaps he wouldn't go back to school next year. Not because, as Jason dreamed, they might be playing full-time, but because he might be in London. He hadn't said anything to the group or to his dad, but the idea still made him feel miserable every time he thought about it. His mum never mentioned it and he was determined not to ask, but he sensed that she still hadn't made up her mind. He often caught her sitting, staring into space, as if she were trying to work something out.

They played their first gig at 'Goliath's' and, despite the fact that they all missed the extra depth that Dave's keyboards had given their sound, it went well. They recognized many of their old fans in the audience that packed out the club, but the summer season had already started and there were a lot of young people who were obviously on holiday. The sound in the club was excellent, and there was a really professional lighting system which helped them. But they knew that the ovation they got at the end of the show was mainly because they were playing at the top of their form. His dad had set up a stall by the door and by the end of the evening he'd sold 187 copies of the single.

"Not bad for a start," he said afterwards, "but now we gotta get it in the charts and you lot can 'elp. Get everyone you know to buy it and write letters requesting it to the local radio – I've made sure they've got a copy. Write the letters yourself, if you 'ave to. I've already written twenty meself and put other people's names and addresses on them. Tomorrow, Buddy and me are gonna start on the record shops."

The next day Buddy sat in the truck and watched his dad go into 'Victory Discs' carrying a large bottle of scotch. Ten minutes later he came out grinning and gave Buddy a big thumbs-up as he crossed the road.

"Some people'd sell their grannies if you offered 'em a little present. Worked like a charm – he'll take fifty and put the poster in the window."

He went back with the records and a moment later he appeared in the shop window, sticking up the poster he'd made. In big red letters it said, 'On Sale Here – Buddy and the Bosses' Single'.

They moved on to the other shop that the paper used to make up the chart, and his dad did exactly the same thing. The manager of 'In A Spin' was only too willing to put up a poster and take fifty copies on a sale or return basis.

"Told me 'e always tries to support local bands," his dad said, "but he couldn't keep 'is eyes off the bottle of whisky on the counter. They're all bent. Right, now we gotta make sure people start buying."

They drove back to 'Victory Records' and during the next hour his dad persuaded ten young passers-by to accept his money to go in and buy the single. Then they went back to 'In A Spin' and did the same thing there. They had a break for lunch then spent another hour outside each of the shops.

"Well, that's forty-five records in one day. I reckon that's enough to make you about number twenty in the charts already," his dad said as they drove back to the breakers yard.

At six, when the yard closed, he used his key to get into the office and started ringing the radio station every ten minutes to request the record. He tried to sound different each time and Buddy almost had hysterics listening to him as he changed accents and raised or lowered his voice.

"That's enough for tonight – don't want 'em to get suspicious. You can ring later from 'ome – get your mum to phone, too. I 'ope the rest of the group's doing the same."

They walked through the industrial estate together and almost all the way back to Buddy's road before his dad stopped.

"Blimey, forgot where I was going. Old habits. For a moment I thought . . . Anyway, I'm off to see Dawn. Ain't seen 'er for ages – says she's fed up wiv this music stuff. As bad as your mum. By the way, say 'ello to 'er for me."

He turned and walked away quickly.

Buddy didn't have the chance to pass the message on because she wasn't home. She'd left a message that she would be late back so he made a sandwich and tuned into the radio. Every time the DJ began to announce a record he held his breath, hoping it would be 'Torn In Half', but it never was. He rang the station and requested it, then rang Glenn but he was out so he called the twins. He told Mike about the record shops and asked what he and Jason had done.

"We've been in contact with everyone we know, telling them to go out and buy it. Jas went down to 'In A Spin' and bought one, but I didn't have the nerve. But I've rung the radio a couple of times and . . ."

Mike broke off and Buddy heard him call "What?" An instant later his voice came down the phone again. "It's on – Jason says they're playing it!"

Buddy dropped the phone and ran into the kitchen. He switched his radio on and 'Torn In Half' came blasting out at him. He grabbed the radio and dashed back to the phone. When he picked it up he heard the song coming down the line, mixed with the sound of Mike and Jason laughing and whooping.

"It's us!" he yelled and then joined in the laughter.

He went to bed before his mum got home and although he heard her moving round the house next morning, she'd gone to work by the time he got up. She had left another note, though.

It said simply, 'Buddy, please be in when I get home. I've got to talk to you. Love, Mum.'

24

His dad was out that day delivering car parts, so there was nothing to distract Buddy from his worries. He went round to see Mike and Jason but their constant talk about the future of the group only made it worse. He couldn't tell them that perhaps there wasn't going to be a future.

He was sitting on the floor of his bedroom playing his old guitar when his mum got home. She came in and sat on his bed. He felt so nervous that he kept gently strumming chords as she started to speak.

"I know you don't want to talk about this London thing, but we've got to. Thursday is the last day I can hand in my notice if we're going."

He strummed the guitar harder, sliding his hand up and down the fret-board and playing random chords that clashed against each other.

"Buddy, please talk to me."

He went on strumming, striking the strings sharply with the plectrum so that the notes stabbed out in silence.

"For God's sake, put that damn thing down a minute," she shouted.

He struck another chord then slowly propped the guitar up against the wall and stared coldly at her.

"Buddy, I want what's best for both of us."

"Oh yeah? Best for me? You just want to live with that Mandell creep. And you want me to say yes so you can feel OK about it."

He wanted a row. He wanted to hurt her, wanted to be able to shout and say things that would make her cry. But she didn't snap back. She stayed silent for ages then shook her head sadly and spoke quietly.

"I thought you understood things better than that. How do you think I feel when I hear that song of yours?"

A flush of shame hit him. It had never occurred to him that she had listened to what the song was about. His dad hadn't – he always called it "that love song". Well, in a way, it was a love song; but it was also an angry, accusing song and she had seen that.

She went on, and every one of her quietly spoken words cut through him in a way that a row never could have done. "See if you can write a song about this, Buddy. I've been with your dad since I was seventeen and I'm caught up with him whether I like it or not. But we can't live together, not day in and day out – you've seen that – and anyway, he's got someone else. I love you but you're nearly grown up. In a couple of years you'll go off and start living your own life. Then there's Adrian. He doesn't mean as much to me as you two, but he's helped me, been good to me. And he wants me. If I go with him, I lose you and your dad. If I stay here, I end up alone. Torn In Half – you don't know what it means."

He had been wrong about Julius and now he'd been wrong about his mum. As she closed the door behind her, he picked up his guitar and started strumming it, but when he realized he was playing the chords of 'Torn In Half' he put it down again. She shouldn't feel like that. It was all right for Julius to be lost and confused, but not his mum. She was grown up and . . . And what? He'd always imagined that when you got to a certain age everything suddenly became clear and you knew what you wanted and you knew what to do. And yet, here was his mum – and probably his dad . . . probably all the adults he knew – as lost and confused as he and Julius were. It was a terrible thought.

Did it mean that nobody was ever sure of what they were doing, or where they were going? His dad was always talking about success, about making it. Buddy wanted that too – wanted to make it with the group and get to the top. But supposing he got there and it wasn't enough? At one time he would have given anything to be in a group and make a record. Well, he'd done that and now he wanted more. Did all the wanting and searching just go on and on – no matter what you did, or how old you got? Somewhere, surely, there was something to stop you feeling lost and confused.

'Torn In Half' had always been his song but when they played it the following evening at 'Goliath's' he couldn't stop thinking about his mum. The song would never be the same again. When his dad burst into the dressing-room and showed them the local record chart, Buddy was almost unhappy to see the record at number seven. If only it had been another song . . .

"It's probably all the ones you bought," he said moodily.

"Blimey, what a misery-guts. Look, there's an article, too," his dad said, pointing to the headline 'Local Group in Chart'. "Just wait – wiv all the radio time it's getting, it'll be number one next week."

The others were thrilled, but Buddy couldn't join in the excitement. He had thought almost non-stop about what his mum had said, and he had made up his mind. If she decided to move to London, he would have to go with her, even if it meant the end of the group.

She was late home on the Thursday. The last light had almost left the sky and he was sitting in his dark bedroom watching for her from the window when Adrian Mandell's car stopped outside. He drew back behind the curtain. The car just stood there.

Five minutes passed. Ten. Fifteen. He was just beginning to wonder if Adrian Mandell was alone – perhaps waiting for something – when the passenger door opened and his mum got out. He watched her push the garden gate then he ran out of the room and down the stairs.

He was waiting on the bottom step when she came in. She looked pale. All evening he'd been trying to work out what to say, how to ask, but he didn't have to.

She put her handbag down, brushed a stray strand of hair from her forehead and said, "I've made up my mind. I'm staying here. I've just told Adrian."

Buddy felt the blood drain from his face. "Because of me?" he asked.

She opened her mouth slightly but her lips trembled and she clenched them together. It was nearly half a minute before she could trust herself to speak again.

"Because of everything."

He should have been happy. It was what he had wanted. But he just felt weak. He sat down on the stairs and she came and sat next to him.

Even this. You got what you wanted and it didn't make you happy. There was always something to take the edge off it. His happiness meant her sadness. She was being brave about it but he knew how much she must hurt.

She put her arm round his shoulders and pulled him towards her. "I don't love Adrian, and that's it. It wouldn't have been fair on anyone. I know it's right like this."

She had proved she was more grown up than he was. She'd thought about other people. For the first time in ages, he held her tight for comfort, like a baby.

He would have liked to spend time with his mum during the next week, but it wasn't possible. Everything suddenly started to take off. Three clubs rang up from nearby towns and booked last-minute gigs. There were anxious to have the group because they were in the charts so his dad was able to charge nearly twice the normal fee. There was another newspaper interview and a live half-hour spot on local radio in which they chatted to a DJ and played four songs. There was even an item about them on a TV review of entertainment in the area. There was a brief film about them on stage at

'Goliath's', then they showed the video and mentioned that it had been made by the group's manager.

All the publicity worked. People on the estate kept stopping Buddy and asking how the group was doing but, more important than that, requests for gigs poured in and in the next chart the record was up to number two. His dad was disappointed that it wasn't number one, but he still put a copy of the charts in with the letter when he sent off the video and the disc to all the record companies.

There was so much work to do setting up the deals and organizing the gigs that his dad fell behind on his deliveries. Buddy and the twins volunteered to help him for a couple of days. They drove in the truck with him from town to town, loading and unloading spare parts at various garages. At the end of the second day, they had just done the last delivery when his dad suddenly pulled up and pointed across the road to a branch of a national chain of record shops.

"If only we could get the record in shops like that . . . C'mon – let's make sure they've 'eard the name."

They went across the road and his dad stopped a young girl and gave her a couple of quid to go in and ask for the record. The girl agreed but Buddy and the twins squirmed with embarrassment, so they went back and sat in the lorry while his dad waited for someone else. A couple of minutes later he went up to a young long-haired man who was just about to go into the shop. They saw him offer the money but the man didn't take it and started waving his hands around as if he were angry. After a moment the man went into the shop and his dad came running across the road and jumped into the truck.

"Strewth," he laughed, starting the engine and roaring away down the street. "I've only gone and tried to bribe the flipping manager of the shop!"

During August they played over twenty gigs and all the hectic activity and the publicity made them feel as if they were really getting somewhere. Then, suddenly, everything started to quieten down. The record stayed at number two for a couple of weeks, then slipped to five, and then disappeared completely from the charts. They still sold quite a number at gigs but by the end of the month the holiday season was over and there were fewer people in the clubs. When they played their final gig at 'Goliath's' the small crowd was mostly made up of local fans, and there was a feeling of anti-climax.

The summer was over.

It had been fun, but they were back where they started. Not a single one of the record companies had reacted to the record and there wasn't another gig lined up until October. It had been a good time but now life was going back to the old routine. Jason was the one who was most depressed.

"God, this place again," he said, as they walked into the common room on the first day back at school.

All morning people came up to them and said they'd seen them on TV and heard the record, but Jason wasn't impressed.

"So what?" he said when Mike told him what people thought. "It's small-time stuff. Hundreds of groups get well-known in their area but they never make it big."

He was right, of course, and as the week wore on and even the people at school stopped talking about the group, Buddy and Mike found themselves agreeing with him that the future looked gloomy.

His dad was still optimistic, though, and he arranged a celebration meal at an Indian restaurant on the Friday. It was raining when Buddy met the others. The wind was blowing in from the sea, rocking the strings of coloured lights, as they walked along the deserted promenade towards the restaurant. They were almost there when his dad drew up in the truck. They stood, muffled up against the wind, with their hair plastered flat by the rain.

"Cor, if your fans could see you now," he said, opening the door and jumping out. "Well, you miserable lot, I've got some good news. 'Ad a phone call yesterday and I've been up London all day talking to Bobby Rosen."

"Who's he?"

"Who's he? Only the managing director of one of the biggest record labels, that's all. Only 'appens to think your record's the best thing since sliced bread. Only wants to see you next week to talk contracts. But if you don't know who 'e is and you can't be bothered . . ."

He dodged inside the restaurant. They stood gaping at each other for a second then barged through the door after him.

The meeting was fixed for early the following Friday evening. They drove up to London in the truck.

"Now don't forget," his dad said after they'd found a parking space and were crossing the square towards the large building, "let me do the talking, right? They're all sharks, this lot – but I know 'ow to 'andle them. And, by the way, I'm just your manager, right? I ain't told 'em Buddy's me son."

They pushed through the glass swing doors marked 'XS Records' and into the thickly-carpeted lobby. While his dad went over to the reception desk, the others looked at the framed gold discs lining the wall.

"Fifth floor, mate," his dad said to the man who operated the lift. Then, as the doors closed, he added, "This lot 'ere are gonna be your next superstars."

The man raised his eyebrows and gave them all a bored look to show that he wasn't impressed.

For some reason Buddy had pictured Bobby Rosen as a young man with jewellery and trendy clothes, and he was surprised to see the bald old man who stood up behind his desk when they walked into the office.

"Bobby, 'ow are you doing?" his dad shouted.

"Hello, Mr Clark, I didn't realize you were coming, too," Mr Rosen said, walking forward with a slight limp, and shaking his dad's hand.

"What, and leave my boys wiv an old crook like you?" his dad laughed. "You must be joking."

Mr Rosen smiled thinly then turned and shook hands with the group. Buddy almost winced as his hand was squeezed painfully in a fierce grip that seemed calculated to hurt.

"Well, do sit down," Mr Rosen said, perching on the edge of his huge desk. "I'll be very brief. We've heard your record and we think you've got potential. You're young and very raw but, with time, you might get somewhere. In the light of that, we're prepared to offer you an option. What that means is that we'll sign you up for a year and see how you develop. Those of you at school can stay there. This is a tough business and you'd be well advised to have something to fall back on if you fail at this. In the meantime XS Records will take you over and do all we can to bring the best out of you. We'll give you studio time to get used to recording, and we'll see about fixing you up with some important gigs that'll get you noticed – perhaps even a support spot on a big name tour if the timing is right.

"It'll be a year in which you can write and record new material and improve your playing until you're really ready to be launched. If we're pleased with you at the end of that time we'll take up the option and sign you; if not we'll shake hands and go our ways. Well, that's our offer – what do you think of it?"

His dad didn't think much of it, and said so. While he went on, saying that the group was ready to start recording at once and demanding that they should have the chance to make an album and get it out in time for the big sales at Christmas, Buddy watched Mr Rosen's face. He sat patiently, without a flicker of emotion, simply shaking his head at every demand, and all the time it was obvious that he was thinking of something else.

At last he stood up and said, "Terry – can I call you Terry? Good. Terry, before we go any further I'd like to show you some of the facilities we'd be offering you. Let's all pop down to the studio."

He didn't wait for them to agree, but led the way out of the office and down the stairs.

"As you'll see, Terry," he said, pushing open a door and ushering them into a huge control booth, "we've got the most sophisticated technology there is."

They walked past rows and rows of tape machines and electronic equipment towards a man who was sitting at the end of an enormous recording console.

"This is Eric. Eric, do me a favour and show my friend Terry some of the things we can do in here. I just want to show these lads the studio. You'll be able to see us through here, Terry." Mr Rosen tapped on the window.

Buddy and the others followed him out of another door and on to the studio floor. There were three grand pianos and two drum-kits standing in the middle of a huge array of microphones. Glenn picked up a drumstick and gently tapped a cymbal.

"Wow, what a set-up," he said.

"Quite something, isn't it?" Mr Rosen said, then turned to the control booth. "Can you hear us, Terry?"

Buddy saw his dad lean towards the plate glass and raise his thumb with a big smile.

"Eric, why don't you give Terry some headphones and let him listen to some stuff we've been recording today."

The man handed some headphones to his dad and set one of the tape machines running.

"Right, Eric, kill the mikes in here, please," Mr Rosen said. The man gave a thumbs-up and flicked a switch.

"Good," Mr Rosen said, and turned to them. "Now you've heard our offer, but I've got one further condition. I don't know how much you know about your manager but since I met him last week we've found out that he's got a police record."

Buddy's heart lurched as the others darted looks at him.

"Naturally," Mr Rosen continued, "that makes us unwilling to make deals with him. As I say, we think you have great promise and we'd love to take out an option on you. But we want you without him. It's up to you. We'll let you have a couple of weeks to think it over."

He smiled kindly at them. "And now I think we'd better go back inside, don't you?"

25

Mike phoned a couple of days later to say that he'd called a meeting of the group at eight o'clock that evening. Buddy deliberately arrived late at the twins' house so that the others could talk before he got there – perhaps say things that they wouldn't want to say in front of him.

As soon as he got into Mike's bedroom it was obvious that they had already started the discussion and that sides had been taken. Glenn was crouching on the floor scowling at Jason and Mike who were sitting side by side on the bed.

"Well?" Buddy said, going over and leaning against the wall next to Glenn.

"I've already told them," Glenn said, nodding at the twins. "I don't care if Terry's robbed the Bank of England, he's been a great manager for us. He's put up money, found us gigs, got us a record in the charts – and I think we ought to stick with him."

"Nobody's denied he's been a good manager," Jason said.

"So?" Glenn asked aggressively.

"So, XS won't take us if he's our manager," Mike said. "And they're offering us a good deal. Jas and I have talked it over with our parents and they think we should take it – especially as it means we can finish school."

"School. Parents," Glenn sneered. "What about the group? What about loyalty to Terry?"

And that was the pattern it took for nearly an hour – Glenn arguing one way and the twins arguing the other. Buddy stayed out of it. A dull, throbbing pain started to squeeze the inside of his skull and, as the room got stuffier, waves of sickness swept through his stomach. At last he couldn't stand it any longer so he told them he was ill and that he had to go. As soon as he got outside, the cool night air revived him. He leaned against the garden wall, breathing deeply, then started for home, feeling the tense pain in his head fade away. He was halfway down the street when Glenn caught up with him.

"I couldn't stick it, either," Glenn panted. "They started talking about ringing Dave to see what he thinks so I just left. He ain't even a proper member of the group."

"He played on the record," Buddy said. "It's only fair he should have a say."

"Fair! What's fair about kicking your dad out after all he's done? I think you and me ought to quit – see how far they get without us. XS won't want 'em, that's for sure."

"Break up the group?"

"Why not? Start again – you and me. We'll find some other people."

"But the group's good together, Glenn. We might not get it right again. And supposing we made it with another group. How do we know that other record labels won't turn us down because of my dad?"

As he said it, the full truth of what he was saying hit him. Perhaps they would never get anywhere in music while he was their manager. He groaned. "Oh God, I just don't know what to do."

"Nor me. It ain't fair!" Glenn swiped the top of a parked car they were passing and a small dog sprang up inside and yapped at them all the way down the road.

"Oh well, I'm going home," Glenn said when they reached the main road. "Listen, mate, someone's gonna have to talk to Terry. I'll do it if you like."

Buddy shook his head. "No – it's got to be me. Thanks for sticking up for him back there."

Glenn shrugged, then gave him a friendly punch on the arm and headed away down the hill.

The problem went round and round in Buddy's head and there seemd no way out. He would have to choose between the group and his dad. And either way it meant that he had to talk to him, so the sooner the better.

He went round to the caravan the following evening and his dad didn't make it easy. He was so happy and full of plans about what he was going to make XS Records promise to do that Buddy couldn't bring himself to say anything. He kept looking at the clock and telling himself that he'd start to speak at quarter past, or twenty-five minutes past, but each time his nerve failed him.

His dad was just making some coffee and Buddy was watching the clock tick towards the new deadline of ten to nine when there was the faint sound of breaking glass.

"What was that?" his dad asked, putting down the spoon and opening the caravan door. He listened a moment and was about to close it again when there came another distant crash and a faint cry of pain.

"The office," his dad said, and jumped out into the darkness.

Buddy dived after him, banging his elbow on the door frame as he went. His dad was halfway towards the office already but as Buddy sprinted after him along the muddy track he saw him stop. As he caught up with him, his dad put his finger to his lips. There was another cry of pain, much louder now, and his dad tip-toed forward, looking to right and left as he went. They had nearly reached the wooden building when he bent down and picked up an iron bar that was lying next to a wrecked car. He signalled to Buddy to stay where he was, climbed the steps up to the office, and slowly turned the door handle. As his dad opened the door and stepped inside, Buddy dashed up the stairs after him.

Two big men spun round and faced them. Behind the men, Buddy caught a glimpse of Des King. His face was bleeding and he was standing with his hands trapped in the top drawer of a filing cabinet. His smashed glasses lay at his feet.

One of the men stepped forward and the light gleamed on the blade of the knife he was holding.

His dad swung the iron bar in front of him then spoke softly. "I wouldn't if I were you." He swung the bar again, menacingly, then reached back and grabbed Buddy by the coat, pulling him away from the door. "These gentlemen are leaving. That's right, innit?"

The two men glanced at each other, then at the door.

His dad moved to the wall, pulling Buddy with him so that there was a clear way out. He lowered the iron bar and the men edged forward, keeping their eyes on him all the way. At the door, the one with the knife looked back to where Des King was standing.

"I hope you got the message, anyway, Des," he called, then followed the other one down the steps.

His dad kicked the door to, and they listened as the running footsteps faded away. Car doors slammed. Tyres screeched and a car drove off.

Des King trembled all the way as Buddy and his dad led him slowly across the yard to the caravan. He moaned softly as they sat him down gently on one of the bunk beds, then he sank back against the wall with his eyes closed.

"I'll get some water," his dad said and ran outside.

Buddy stood staring at King. His nose and mouth were bleeding, but the worst damage was to his hands which hung limply between his legs. The fingers were swollen and blood was oozing from the dark bruises that were spreading around the knuckles.

"Who were they, Des?" his dad asked as he came back in with a basin of water. He grabbed a towel, dipped it in the water, then squatted down and began gently wiping away the blood on King's face.

"Couple of heavies from London," King mumbled through his mangled lips. "People up there, trying to put the frightners on me."

He gave a snort of laughter and winced. "Did a good job, too. Scared me stiff. I think my fingers are broken. Funny thing – couldn't stop thinking about my dad. Ever tell you about him, Terry?"

"No, what?" his dad asked, dipping the towel in the water again before continuing to dab it softly round King's nose.

"Ducked and dived all his life, he did. Always after money for us lot at home. Never made much – didn't have the talent for it like me. Then they told him he had cancer. Ooh, that hurts."

"Sorry, Des," his dad said and dipped the towel again.

Buddy saw the blood on the towel swirl around and colour the water.

"Told him he had two months to live. Just like that. Know what he did? Put an ad in the paper – said he was dying and that he was willing to pass on messages from people to their dead relatives in the next world." King chuckled then winced again. "Guess what. He got nearly two hundred takers at a quid a throw. Fair bit of money in those days. Crafty blighter – best scam he ever thought of. It tided us over for nearly a year after he'd gone."

There was a silence when King finished his story. His dad dabbed once more at the blood, then rocked back on his heels.

"Some bloke, your dad," he said.

"Yeah, some bloke," King said and opened his eyes. "Can you get me home, Terry? Don't want to go to a hospital. My wife'll ring our doctor – he can keep his mouth shut."

"'Course. Give us an 'and, Buddy."

They lifted King to his feet and led him to the door.

"Funny, eh?" King said as they got him outside. "The whole time they were doing me over, all I could think of was my poor old man."

It was a hard job getting him into the truck because he couldn't use his hands to haul himself in but, at last, they managed to ease him up and on to the seat. Buddy got up beside him. When the truck moved away King started to slump sideways and Buddy put his arm round his shoulders to steady him. His dad drove slowly but at every bump King groaned. Buddy felt him tense with pain.

"Nearly there, Des," his dad said.

"Yeah, nearly there," King's voice was blurred. "Mary'll see me all right. Mary'll look after me. She's a good woman. I'm a lucky man. Need a good woman."

They drew into the drive of a large house and the tyres crunched on the gravel as his dad stepped on the brakes. Buddy held on to Des King while his dad got out and came round to open the door. Then, together, they lifted him out and stood him up.

"Mary'll look after me," he said again. They turned him round and walked him slowly towards the steps.

"How's that Dawn of yours, Terry?" King asked suddenly, stopping at the bottom step.

"Don't see much of her," his dad said. "Come on, Des, let's get you up them steps."

King shrugged them away. "No, I'll do it on my own."

They watched as he staggered up the four steps towards the door.

"Need a good woman, Terry," he said, swaying slightly as he looked over his shoulder. "You're the best friend I got. Don't like to see you on your own."

He leaned heavily against the doorframe and a bell rang in the house. He raised his arm painfully and jerked it stiffly to show they should go. As his dad backed the truck out of the drive, the front door opened and Buddy saw a pair of woman's arms close round Des King's back.

His dad pulled up outside the breakers yard, yanked on the handbrake and switched off the engine. He leaned back in the seat, put his hands behind his head, and let out a long breath. For almost ten minutes they sat there, silently staring through the windscreen at the row of lights stretching away down the street, then Buddy leaned over and opened his door.

As he stepped on to the pavement, he knew he had to say it. It was the worst possible moment, but he couldn't bear to keep it bottled up any longer.

"Dad," he said, sitting down on the edge of the cab and fixing his eyes on the corrugated iron gates of the yard. "I've got to tell you something."

He stayed there, staring at the gates, not daring to look round and see his dad's face, while the whole story poured out. What Bobby Rosen had said. The discussion with the group. How Glenn had stood up for him. Everything.

It came out fast and he wasn't even aware that tears had started to roll down his cheeks until he had finished and felt the cold wind blow across the tracks they'd made on his face. He brushed them away and sniffed. There was no sound or movement from behind him, and Buddy tried to control the shivers that started to shake his shoulders.

"Never ends, does it?" his dad said at last. "Once you bin in nick they never let you forget it."

Buddy clenched his fists and beat his knuckles together.

"So, what you gonna do?" his dad asked.

Suddenly he knew. What a waste of time it had been worrying about what to do. He couldn't let his dad down, ever. Not for some stupid group – not for anything.

"I'm going to start a new group with Glenn. And we want you as the manager." He spun round, able to face him at last. "Dad, when you were in prison, I made a vow. I swore I'd never make you unhappy – never. And I won't."

His dad had been leaning forward with his arms on the steering wheel but now he sat up and looked out of the windscreen. After a moment he started to slide along the seat towards Buddy and as he reached the door, and the lamplight fell on him, there was a smile on his face. He reached out and ruffled Buddy's hair, like in the old days.

"You and me together, eh?" He winked. "You're a good kid, Buddy, and you couldn't make me un'appy if you tried. Go 'ome. Go on."

He jumped out of the truck, pulled Buddy's nose and tapped him under the chin. "You 'eard me – 'ome. It's late."

All next day Buddy made sure he avoided the twins because he wanted to talk to Glenn before he told them anything. At the end of school he deliberately left without going back to the common room but when he turned the corner at the bottom of the school steps he saw them. They were standing talking to Glenn next to his milk-float.

"Here he is," Glenn said as Buddy walked up to them.

"What're you doing?" Buddy asked.

Glenn looked at the others then handed him a large brown envelope. "Terry was waiting for me at the depot when I got back from my round. He gave me this."

Buddy tipped up the envelope and pulled out the contents. There was the contract they had signed, torn in half, and a note written on Des King's notepaper.

Buddy read the scrawly writing. "I've rung XS and told them you're going to sign with them. Here's to your first number one. Cheers, Terry."

"Some bloke, your dad," Glenn said as Buddy bundled the envelope back into his hand and started to run.

His dad wasn't in the caravan when Buddy arrived panting at the breakers yard. He ran over to the office and found him sitting behind Des King's desk with his feet up.

"Dad, why did you do it?" he managed to gasp.

"Funny thing, you making that vow while I was in nick," his dad said, "'cos I made one while I was in there, an' all. Do you know what mine was? I vowed I wouldn't never do nuffing to stand in your way. That sort of makes us quits, don't it?"

26

'Buddy and the Bosses' signed the option with XS Records at the end of September. The whole thing was very formal and even Glenn had to have his parents with him when he signed. Buddy's signature had to be counter-signed by his dad.

"Sure it's good enough for you, Bobby?" he said sarcastically.

Mr Rosen clapped him on the back and smiled, "Don't be like that, Terry. I'd like a word with you after this is over."

Buddy went down to the lobby, said goodbye to the others, and waited for his dad. He looked round at all the gold discs and wondered if one day there would be one of 'Buddy and the Bosses' hanging on the wall. It wouldn't be for ages, of course. Mr Rosen had told them that it would be at least nine months before they would think of releasing a record. In the meantime, they were to go on practising and writing new material. He said he'd fix up a week in the studio in December when they could experiment with their new songs and that he would probably arrange some gigs at Christmas time, but all that seemed a long time off.

The lift door slid open and his dad stepped out.

"What a creep!" he said as they pushed through the swing doors on to the pavement. "Offered me five hundred quid. 'As recompense, Terry, don't you know – it's a fair offer.' I told 'im to stuff his money. Five hundred? Bloomin' cheek. Cost us about six times that wiv the discs and videos and stuff."

"It's better than nothing," Buddy said, feeling guilty about all the money his dad had spent. "Anyway, we'll pay you back when we start earning."

"Nah," his dad said, putting his arm round Buddy's shoulder. "Most of it was Des's money, anyway, and 'e could drop ten grand down the drain and not notice it. Besides, as 'e keeps telling me – 'e owes me. Walk over 'ot coals for me, if I asked 'im. 'Ere, the boozers are open, let's go an 'ave a drink to celebrate."

He didn't see much of his dad over the next six weeks. There was a lot of school work to do and almost every day he also met the group to try out ideas for new songs. Apart from that, Des King had gone away for a holiday so his dad was busy running the yard and, in the evenings, he had started seeing a lot of the Video King. This meant that Buddy stayed at home more, talking to his mum about the changes at her office since Mr Mandell had left. She was practically running things now. She often brought papers home and spent the evening working, so he tried to make things easier by doing jobs around the house.

One evening, the kitchen sink got blocked. Buddy fetched some of his dad's tools and started to undo the trap on the waste pipe. He was lying directly underneath it, wrenching at the nut with a spanner, when the trap opened and showered him with dirty water and muck that had got caught in the pipe. Water spilled all over the floor. The noise brought his mum running into the kitchen. He was just wiping the filth off his sweater when the back door opened and his dad walked in. It was over a year since he'd been in the house and for a moment they all looked at each other awkwardly.

Then his dad noticed the water and laughed. "Cor blimey, I see the mechanical genius 'as been at it. Couldn't stick a drawing pin in the wall, 'e couldn't. You should give me a bell if you want fings like that done, Carol."

His mum blushed as his dad took off his jacket, rolled up his sleeves, and ducked under the sink. Buddy dashed upstairs to change his sweater and by the time he got down his dad had already fixed it.

"Shouldn't 'ave any problems wiv that," his dad said, slipping his jacket on.

"Thanks, Terry," his mum said. There was a pause then she asked him if he'd like some coffee.

"No, ta – I gotta go. Only dropped round to tell you me news, really. Bin up to London today wiv Alan – you know, the Video King. We 'ad a chat wiv the bigwigs up Arctic Records – one of the labels I sent the stuff to in the summer. Anyway, they're setting up their own video studios now, and they wanted to talk to me and Alan about working wiv 'em."

"Dad, that's great," Buddy shouted.

"Yeah, well, it ain't certain yet, but it looks pretty 'opeful. We gotta go up again next week. Even told 'em about you know what. Didn't want 'em finding out and turning me down like your lot. They said they didn't give a toss about the past. So who knows. Anyway, I thought I'd just tell you. Well, better be off."

He walked to the kitchen door. Buddy wanted to stop him but he didn't know what to say.

"Terry," his mum called as he opened the door. "I . . . I'm really pleased for you."

"Yeah, ta."

Buddy saw the brief glance they exchanged and it gave him the courage to speak.

"Listen – we ought to celebrate. And it's my seventeenth birthday next Tuesday. So I'm inviting you out – both of you – to have something to eat. Please. I'll pay."

"Listen to money-bags," his dad laughed. "OK. Carol?"

Buddy looked at her. "Please, Mum – we never spend my birthday together. Just this once."

She nodded.

"Right. Next Tuesday, then," his dad said. "Nuffin' posh, mind – don't want to dress up an' all that."

"No, that pizza place on the front or somewhere like that."

His mum groaned. "That's the trouble with you two – no style, no class. Why not that new French restaurant?"

"Oh Gawd, no – I 'ate them sort of places. Never know which knife and fork you 'ave to use."

"I'll show you," his mum insisted.

His dad looked doubtful but then smiled. "OK, why not? If money-bags 'ere can afford it."

"'Course I can," Buddy said. "Right, that's fixed."

He walked to the street with his dad and they stood on the pavement, not speaking, but happy just to be together in familiar surroundings.

"Oh well . . ." his dad said at last.

"I really hope the video thing works out," Buddy said, touching his dad's arm in farewell.

"Don't you worry about that, mate. You know me – I'm lucky. See yer."

He started off down the road – the same jaunty old walk that Buddy could always pick out in any crowd. He'd only gone a few yards, though, when he slipped and looked down.

"Urgh," he said. "Now look – all over me best suedes."

He cupped his hands to the sides of his mouth and yelled along the dark street. "You filthy lot – ought to keep your dogs under control!"

He began scuffing his shoe from side to side on the edge of the pavement and then suddenly chuckled. He looked back at Buddy. "Told you I was lucky, didn't I."

He started to laugh. He was still laughing when he reached the corner. He waved to Buddy and disappeared from view, but his laughter echoed back along the street.

Torn in Half

You're telling me your stories,
You're handing me a line,
You're giving me your point of view
But you never think of mine.
You tell me that you love me,
You say I ought to laugh.
Why is it that you just can't see
That I am torn in half?
I try to laugh
But I'm torn in half.

You say you can't be happy
With the way things used to be
That things have changed for you now
So they must change for me.
You say that I'll get used to it
That nothing ever lasts.
Yes, that is your excuse for it
But I am torn in half.
No, nothing lasts
And I'm torn in half.

The whole world is divided,
Seems set to break apart,
And now what you've decided
Is going to break my heart.

You made some vows a while ago
Before I came along,
But now I really need you
You think those vows are wrong.

You're headed for a different life
You've got a brand new path
The things you've done cut like a knife
And leave me torn in half.

You've got a brand new path
But I'm torn in half.

Brain Train

Someone's looking through my eyes,
My mouth is talking, telling lies,
My head is filled with strangers
Like a country filled with spies.
One voice says 'Just be happy',
Another says, 'No, just be sad'.
Both these voices are inside me
Till I feel I'm going mad.

CHORUS

Who's the driver on this brain train?
Who can hear and feel and see?
Who's the driver on this brain train?
'Cos I'm sure it isn't me.

Have you ever tried not thinking?
It's not an easy thing to do.
Who controls what you are thinking?
You'll find out it isn't you.
Try to make yourself feel one thing
And your brain will just rebel
Try to think that you're in heaven
And your brain will make it hell.

CHORUS

Where's the guard? Where's the station?
Stop this train, I scream and shout.
But I'm stuck inside this carriage
Gotta ride this journey out.

Gotta ride with this computer
Working away inside my mind,
But will I learn to press the right keys
Before I crash right off this line?

CHORUS

Nothing Serious

Strange that they all meant so much less to you
Those beautiful moments that we shared.
And sad to think that every time you held me close
Deep down inside you never cared.
I believed every single word you said to me,
I believed every promise in your kiss.
I know now they were lies you were telling me,
But they're lies that I'm really gonna miss.

Oh but love's nothing special or mysterious
Just breaks your heart apart,
Makes burning teardrops start,
No, love doesn't count – it's nothing serious.

I tell my friends I've already gotten over it,
I never let them see that I'm in pain,
Like I never let you see me near your house at night
Standing waiting for you in the pouring rain.
Even now I still hope that you'll come back to me
That those words of goodbye were never real,
That maybe tomorrow you will change your mind
And put an end to this misery I feel.

Oh but love's nothing special or mysterious
Just burns you every day
And hurts in every way,
No, love doesn't count – it's nothing serious.

I can't play records that we used to listen to,
I can't visit places where we used to go,
I can't read letters that you sent to me –
Every word of them hits me like a blow.
Sometimes I hate you for the things you've done
But the hatred never seems to last
My present and my future are so empty now
Because my heart is still living in the past.

Oh but love's nothing special or mysterious
Just kills off happiness,
Fills you with emptiness,
No, love doesn't count – it's nothing serious.